animals in film

LOCATIONS

series editors:
AL REES AND BARRY CURTIS

LOCATIONS is a new series of thematic books examining contemporary genres and hybrids in national and international cinema. Each book contains numerous black and white images and a fresh critical exploration of aspects of film's relationship with other media, major themes within film, or different aspects of national film cultures.

on release:

projected cities
STEPHEN BARBER

in production:

mad, bad and dangerous:
the scientist and the cinema
CHRISTOPHER FRAYLING

animals in film

JONATHAN BURT

REAKTION BOOKS

Reaktion Books Ltd
79 Farringdon Road,
London EC1M 3JU, UK

www.reaktionbooks.co.uk

First published 2002

Printed and bound in Great Britain by Cromwell Press, Trowbridge, Wiltshire

British Library Cataloguing in Publication Data:

Burt, Jonathan
    Animals in Film. – (Locations)
    1. Animals in motion pictures 2. Photography of animals
    I. Title
    7912.4'3662

ISBN 1 86189 131 8

contents

'Leave the rooster story, that's human interest' – *His Girl Friday*

'Don't lose your head.'
'My *what?*'
'Your head.'
'I've got my head; I've lost my leopard.' – *Bringing up Baby*

prologue

In October 1949 the filmmakers Michael Powell and Emeric Pressburger wrote a letter to *The Times* about the production of their forthcoming film *Gone to Earth*, based on the novel by Mary Webb.[1] The filmmakers complained that they were being prevented from completing their film by the action of the British Field Sports Society (BFSS) who had decreed that no master of foxhounds should lend his pack for the final scenes, given that the film would encourage anti-hunting sentiment. The climax of the film sees Hazel, the heroine of the movie, running across the landscape carrying her pet fox while pursued by hounds and huntsmen only to fall down a disused mineshaft to her death. 'It is surely absurd to create propaganda out of a work of art and to create most undesirable publicity over a book which has become a minor classic', wrote Powell and Pressburger.

The story itself was a tale of a woman caught between the love of two men, the minister and the local squire. Far from propaganda, the film was a piece of highly theatrical melodrama combining some beautiful landscape photo-

Hazel, the heroine of
Gone to Earth and her
pet fox being hunted
down in Powell and
Pressburger's 1950 film
of Mary Webb's novel.

The two outcasts in
Gone to Earth.

graphy alongside an exaggerated exploitation of the garish colours of Technicolor. For instance, a series of carefully gradated scarlets and browns thread together the dress of the adulteress, worn by Hazel after she has left her husband for the local squire; the huntsman's coat; the russet of the fox's coat and the dark sepia tones of the domestic interiors that reflect the claustrophobia of the world indoors. In the same way the name Hazel alludes to the outdoors, the hazel tree, and the colour of the fox. The fox, like Hazel herself, carries contradictory connotations: it is at once pet, object of desire and vermin, an object of disgust – both half-tame and half-wild. Furthermore, the creature is also figured as the focus of a long-running social conflict over issues of cruelty.[2] However, there are no graphic scenes of cruelty in the film, such as a kill, that might turn a viewer against foxhunting if the viewer were not already opposed. Even the fox was subject to a certain artifice, given that the filmmakers could not find enough trained foxes for the shoot – they needed three – and experimented with tying fox's brushes to corgi dogs.[3] But, in opposing the depiction of hunting scenes, the British Field Sports Society was showing some prescience, particularly concerning the potential power of animal visual imagery to arouse impassioned responses. It was not the first film to have caused such concerns. In 1942 the Walt Disney film *Bambi* (1942) excited considerable debate in the United States, and was labelled by the hunting lobby as anti-hunting propaganda: 'the worst insult ever offered in any form to American sportsmen'.[4] In this book I will show that when it comes to animals, the line between art and 'propaganda' can be very fine indeed.

Animal imagery in film has a peculiar status in that, despite a general awareness of the contrivances of the medium, audiences often respond differently to animals or animal-related practices than they do to other forms of imagery. This is not just due to the suspicion, frequently manifested in letters of complaint to film organizations and animal welfare societies, that what is happening on screen is really happening to animals being filmed. It appears that certain kinds of animal imagery, magnified and intensified precisely by the artifice of film, are responded to more emotionally and are therefore less mediated by the judgements that we might normally apply to other kinds of imagery. Like Hazel's pet, Foxy, the animal is caught in an uncertain space between the natural and the contrived. The elements that make up the response to animal imagery appear to compose a similarly ambiguous space. On the one hand, it can be argued that an emotional response to animals is an empathetic and hence a straightforward natural expression of sentiment toward fellow creatures. On the other hand, it can as easily be said that it is film itself that, since its arrival in the mid-1890s, has increasingly influenced the constructions of the animal in the public domain and that the force of the viewer's response to the animal is imbued with the techniques by which film provokes feelings in its audience. The extent to which film is particularly responsible for structuring responses to animals in modernity is difficult to gauge, particularly when generalizing about audience or even public attitudes. This is a particular problem given that almost no systematic research has been conducted on audience responses to animal imagery from the perspective of a wider cultural concern about animals. However, as I shall argue here, the position of the animal as a visual object is a key component in the structuring of human responses towards animals generally, particularly emotional responses. Rob Block, an animal trainer and the owner of a company called 'Critters of the Cinema', once asked a producer why he was putting a dog in a show. He was told, 'a dog is worth two points in prime time. One point is about 850,000 sets. You do the math.'[5]

Although the animal on screen can be burdened with multiple metaphorical significances, giving it an ambiguous status that derives from what might be described as a kind of semantic overload, the animal is also marked as a site where these symbolic associations collapse into each other. In other words, the animal image is a form of rupture in the field of representation. This vulnerability to ambiguity says a great deal about the position of the animal in our culture. One might be tempted to draw a postmodern conclusion to this by treating the animal as a floating or unstable signifier. However, the fact that the animal image can so readily point beyond its significance on screen to questions about its general treatment or fate in terms of welfare, suggests that the boundaries of film art, as Powell and Pressburger would put it, cannot easily delimit the meaning of the animal within its fictions. In fact, nowadays there would probably be more concern among animal organizations that *Gone to Earth* might encourage a rash of keeping foxes as pets. This rupturing effect of the animal image is mainly exemplified by the manner in which our attention is constantly drawn beyond the image and, in that sense, beyond the aesthetic and semiotic framework of the film. This unavoidable state of being drawn behind the animal's film image is the basis of the conflict over the control of animal imagery. In the instance of *Gone to Earth*, the BFSS's objection and dictat to the foxhunting community was quite specific: they wanted to prevent the making of a powerful set of images that would reflect badly on British foxhunting. Moreover, this problem of the manner in which the animal image constantly points beyond itself is not restricted to high art debates about the treatment of animals. Even playful and contrived forms of animal imagery can be the subject of impassioned objection. In Britain, for example, protests recently caused an advertisement to be withdrawn because it featured an (artificial) bird flying into a pane of glass, like something out of a cartoon. If anything, ethical questions arise most severely at the point at which the line between the fictitious and the *real* animal is most difficult to draw. More complicated still, as the advertisement example proves, that line can also be an irrelevance. Fictional animals, it seems, are just as in need of protection as real ones.

My intention in this book is to understand how this situation arose. How is it that the animal image has come to carry these particular kinds of screen power and why does the relationship between visual imagery and ethics play such a significant part in its history? The answer to such a question is not clear-cut due to a number of factors. Animal imagery has a rupturing effect, both in terms of the way it unavoidably points beyond itself to wider issues and in its capacity to resist or problematize its own meanings on screen. This effect is integral both to the conflicts over animal imagery and the ways in which such imagery is regulated. Both liberating and constraining forces are at work here and these express the complicated links between the various conceptual and political frameworks that contribute to the construction of animal imagery, whether they be humanizing, humane, scientific or commercial. At one level the regulation of animal imagery is determined by the institutions of censorship, animal law and animal-related organizations of all kinds, as well as by the film companies themselves. In addition there are other factors that also have a significant input, such as popular protest, amateur naturalism, public interest in pet-keeping, conservation and education. The *Gone to Earth* example illustrates something of how these parties contribute to the overdetermination of the animal image. The BFSS would probably have justified their position by stating that they sought to prevent the hunting scenes in the film because in the long run they would threaten practices that controlled vermin and hence saved other wildlife. The legislature would have argued that, as long as no animals were harmed in the making of the film, the picture was quite acceptable. Finally, Powell and Pressburger might have felt that this matter of foxes was a minor question, given that their main concern was with the hunting of a woman. Perhaps, they might have said, people should feel more strongly about that.

Seen in this light there are all sorts of faultlines in the animal image that manifest themselves not just in the types of differences sketched out above but in an overall sense of mismatch. A cultural oversensitivity to the treatment of animals on screen appears to sit at odds with a culture that is also heavily dependent on animal exploitation, as many writers have pointed out. Furthermore, considering that the possible themes and scenarios for animal films appear to be quite limited and yet are extraordinarily difficult and time-consuming to make, one may wonder at the cultural investment in the production of such films. Jean-Jacques Annaud's initial synopsis for *L'Ours* (*The Bear*), for instance, read 'A big solitary bear. An orphan bear cub. The hunters in the forest. The animals' point of view.' Despite such apparent simplicity, the resulting film took five years to prepare and included four years spent training the lead bear and finding suitable cubs, nine months to film, using over one million feet of film, and one year to edit.[6] Given that so many, at times contradictory, factors are in play it is hard to reduce the animal image to a single kind of response or meaning – whether it be escapism, romanticization or vicarious thrills – without raising the possibility that there are other elements that constantly counter or complicate such responses.

In the first chapter I explore the implications of this idea of multiplicity and overdetermination for theories about the visuality of the animal in general as well as in film in particular. The second part of this chapter also provides readings of a number of relatively well known films featuring animals to show how visual representation delineates the relations between humans and animals. The second chapter takes a historical overview of the ethics and regulation of animal films and considers the factors that have policed animal imagery, particularly through the history of animal welfare laws and control of the treatment of animals in the film industry. Finally, in the last chapter I look at a number of different kinds of film, such as animal rights videos, family films, documentaries, world cinema, and experimental and surrealist film. My main proposal is that animal imagery does not merely reflect human–animal relations and the position of animals in human culture, but is also used to change them. Indeed, it is this transformative aspect that reveals broader cultural tensions and anxieties about our current treatment of animals and why it is never easy to characterize animal films as merely optimistic or pessimistic, escapist or engaged.

1 film and the history of the visual animal

When I first began working on this book I consulted many general books on film to see what, if anything, they might have to say about animals. Rarely did I find specific index entries for animals. Instead I usually came across 'animation' and 'anthropomorphism'. What is implied by these index entries is that the figure of the animal in film is generally understood in terms of some form of displacement, which, in the case of anthropomorphism and animation, would be largely metaphorical. There are a few recent texts that have proved exceptions to this tendency, though they are mainly confined to natural history and family films, especially Disney, where the animal is an explicit focus of attention; for example Gregg Mitman's *Reel Nature* and Derek Bousé's *Wildlife Films*, both excellent historical studies. Given the significance of animals in visual culture and their extensive appearance in film, the small number of scholarly studies on issues relating to animals in film seems to me the product of a willful blindness.[1] Animals appear, with greater or lesser significance, in all genres of moving film throughout its

Sculpting the lion for the MGM building, c. 1940s.

The mass marketing of a cinematic emblem. Above: 1929. Below: 1933.

history: from wildlife films to Hollywood blockbusters, from scientific films to animation, as well as occurring in surrealist, avant-garde and experimental films, all of which use a multitude of different formats and technologies. Indeed, it is striking how many animals announce film: Pathé's crowing rooster; MGM's lion, a motif also used by Colonel Selig in the early twentieth century; Metro's parrot, which threw the company letters onto the screen; and more recently the flying horse of TriStar.[2]

This project began when I was looking for early-twentieth-century film coverage of London Zoo. My initial motives were simply to see what the Zoo looked like, how people and animals moved in the space of the Zoo at the time. However, it became immediately clear that film did not so much document the animals in the Zoo as present them in a different light.[3] Indeed, film's emphasis on action and event was from a spectator's point of view much closer to the ideal zoo exhibit and provided a contrast to those many hours when

Filming for the Pathé *Secrets of Nature* series at the London Zoo. The series began in 1922.

actual zoo animals do very little and zoo exhibits are minimally eventful. Thus in film the already edited life of the captive animal was edited even further. The fact that the Zoo incorporated different ways of seeing animals not just in its encouragement of film, but also through photography and painting, reflects a more general fact that the history of the visible animal is the product of a mosaic of institutions, technologies and cultural practices, all of which interconnect in various ways.

As I suggested in my preface, there is an important interplay between the diversity of animal imagery, its flexibility of meaning and the manner of its grounding, particularly in areas of ethics. These last are effectively, given the articulation of such ethics through legal and other institutional frameworks, the framework of the social-contractual aspects of human–animal relations. However, this interplay does not form a coherent or easily amalgamated whole. The diversity of animal imagery is one measure of the extent to which film reflects a cultural desire for such imagery and reminds us that the symbolic potential of the animal image is extraordinarily rich. However, this diversity also means that we cannot assume a uniformity of response to animal imagery. To some degree this is inevitable, given the flexibility and variety of cultural codes to be found in most cultures, but it has a particular consequence for those cultures that are especially sensitized to animal issues, notably those with a long tradition of engagement in such issues. In Britain, for instance, the animal has long been an object of cultural conflict in a number of areas, which accounts in part for the strict codes of legislation that govern the appearance of animals on film. This implies, among other things, an acknowledgement of the potentially powerful effects of animal imagery on film. As the French director Georges Franju said, 'When I shot *Les Yeux sans Visage* (1959) I was told: "No sacrilege because of the Spanish market, no nudes because of the Italian market, no blood because of the French market and no martyrized animals because of the English market." And I was supposed to be making a horror film!'[4] Because of the potential emotional impact of animal film imagery in cultures sensitized to animal questions, it is easy to forget that such responses are to a large extent conditioned by specific historical changes in attitudes toward animals, as I shall outline later in the chapter. This does not, incidentally, make the emotions any less real or significant. But, it is easy to lose sight of a historical perspective when concepts of the animal are associated with ideas of naturalness, emotional directness and simplicity; terms which are themselves important cultural constructs.

Just as the global scale of human impact on the world makes it increasingly difficult to separate out biosystems, bodies and technologies, so too is it impossible to disentangle direct and mediated aspects of human–animal relations. In fact, the layers of mediation between animals, humans and nature in the modern world bear some parallels to those that come between film and the worlds that it depicts. Film, the medium of representation in modernity *par excellence*, encapsulates many of those things seen as responsible for alienating man (and animals) from nature: technologization, mass culture, an industry of image reproduction that substitutes for the 'real' world. And yet, film also reasserts the moral importance of the bonds between human and animal. In fact, as I shall describe shortly, there has always been a strong visual component to animal ethics and notions of humane treatment. These issues are often played out in arguments between those who see the naturalness of animals on film as transformative and beneficial, particularly through the idea of pleasurable education or the use of animals as moral exemplars, and those who see film as fundamentally escapist or false.

A brief example to demonstrate the moral significance of animals in film can be found in some of the earliest films starring animals in their own right. The superstar dogs of the 1920s, Strongheart and Rin Tin Tin, achieved phenomenal success. As is well known, Rin Tin Tin had all the trappings of the movie star: a valet, a chef and a limousine as well as a voluminous fan mail.[5] Among the responses to the extraordinary popularity of these dogs was a book, published in 1940 by J. Allen Boone, entitled *Letters to Strongheart*, which is a long paean to the star of films such as the first *White Fang* (1925).[6] Strongheart had been a German-trained military dog and needed to be re-educated in the ways of love and friendship, 'how to be in every way possible that which was rightly himself'.[7] For Boone, dogs such as Strongheart set an example to humans who needed to return to the values of simplicity, goodness and happiness. Dogs should, he noted, be training humans rather than the other way round. However, it was Boone's characterization of Strongheart's acting that neatly conflated the moral virtue of animals, their emotional appeal and the medium of film itself. He perceived that the great quality of Strongheart's acting was precisely that there was no barrier between his good inner nature and his outward manifestation of it. 'People thought they were watching a well-trained dog doing unusual things. What they were really doing, though, was looking through a moving transparency on four legs, and seeing a better universe than the one they had been living in. That is why they were always so eager to come back for more looks.'[8] Thus, the dog as a strip of film embodies the moral potential of film itself. Strongheart does not just stand for a better world but is the medium by which it is made manifest. As we shall see, this kind of thinking is a strand in many animal films throughout the twentieth century.

A counter-current to this belief in the moral good of the exemplary animal can be found not so much in the idea that such moral potential is distinctly limited, but in a more widespread suspicion that animal imagery is unnatural. Where the concept of naturalness invokes a type of truthfulness, this, in turn, reinforces the sense that film images are false by virtue of their cinematic artifice. More generally this view assumes that the relation between nature and culture is an agonistic one. Emotions that are seen as *natural* amongst humans become unnatural when applied to animals. In 1998 Polly Toynbee polemically wrote, in response to the large number of programmes devoted to animals on British televi-

Dogs dressed as cowboys from an MGM short, *Two Barks Brothers* (1931).

Bessie Love with a monkey on the set of Harry Hoyt's *The Lost World* (1925).

Bongo, a gorilla at Twycross Zoo, UK, has a colour television built into his cage, 1971.

sion: 'in a world of human atrocity, this sick obsession with animals has turned into serious decadence'. Stressing the artificiality of emotionalism and the 'strange spasms of public sentiment that have literally no meaning', she declared 'the current vogue for sentimentality about animals will be looked back on in future times as a strange millennial moment.'[9] This tone of austerity and discipline colours a good deal of contemporary critical writing on modern animal imagery, though it derives from a number of different theoretical standpoints. It is not always clear what this austerity is refusing. However, it is based, structurally at least, on assumptions that most human–animal relations in modernity are in various ways wrongful – either sentimental or hollow, or a disconcerting combination of the two. One can trace the strands of this through theories of aesthetics to film itself.

In his book *The Postmodern Animal* Steve Baker argues that 'the modern animal is . . . the nineteenth-century animal (symbolic, sentimental), which has been *made to disappear*.'[10]

In his account of attitudes in postmodern art, ideas of pet-keeping, sentimentality, anthropomorphism and a literal depiction of animal beauty are rejected in favour of bleak and figuratively transgressive versions of the animal. Baker seems to be undecided as to whether this perspective offers a positive rethinking of human–animal relations or whether it intensifies the alienation and disappearance of animals that is seen as the central consequence of modernity. The idea of disappearance echoes John Berger's famous essay, written in 1977, 'Why Look at Animals?', which describes the impact of capitalism on animals as one in which image has come to be substituted for reality.[11] Berger valorizes a view of pre-industrial practical relations with animals that are by implication pre-imagistic and unmediated by forms of representation. This is the fiction of the direct encounter. Measured against this, standard animal imagery will inevitably be considered palliative (substitutive), empty (spectral) and excessive (mass-produced). For these critics the virtuous transparency that Boone sees in Strongheart would inevitably be constituted as merely an emptiness, or at best an illusion.

Reading animals in film through Berger's idealization of direct experience over the image, or through postmodern notions of impossibility in animal representation, makes film one more symptom of the disappearance of the animal in modernity. If the animal is celebrated it is as a sign but not as a body. This thesis is articulated most clearly by Akira Lippit, in his book *Electric Animal*, who follows Berger in his account of the way modernity dissolves the empirical animal into pure spectrality. The consequence of this argument is that film is then merely a palliative, consoling us for a sense of loss and rupture. For these critics, it seems to me, this loss is marked by the arrival of the image itself. Lippit writes, 'Modernity can be defined by the disappearance of wildlife from humanity's habitat and by the reappearance of the same in humanity's reflections on itself: in philosophy, psychoanalysis, and technological media such as telephone, film, and radio.'[12] (It is intriguing to think of wildlife reappearing on the telephone.) In Lippit's extension of Berger's thesis to cinema, the funerary monument to wildlife that was Berger's zoo is paralleled by Lippit's film apparatus: 'Technology and ultimately cinema came to determine a vast mausoleum for animal being.'[13] The views of Berger and Lippit read more like a teleology than a history. Lippit does not really address film in his text except as an abstraction and only briefly mentions a small handful of filmmakers (Muybridge, Marey, Vertov and Eisenstein). This, in fact, is symptomatic of much writing on animals which has a tendency to homogenize both the cultural structures that relate to animals while at the same time making the animal an overly free-floating signifier: 'Animals are incapable of determining or regulating the discourse they put forth: they simply transmit.'[14] Lippit has, in essence, outlined a concept of the animal-machine brought up to date for the radio age. Of course Berger and Lippit have plenty of grounds for pessimism given the recent history of human–animal relations that the rapid rates of species extinction and widespread animal cruelty reveals. But the

A monkey on the set of Frank Buck's *Bring 'Em Back Alive* (1932).

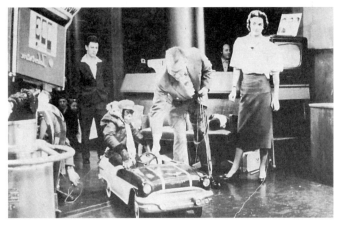

J. Fred Muggs, the monkey who drew new audiences to NBC's *Today* show in the 1950s.

central question here is whether they are correct to imply that the multiplication of the animal image is, ultimately, not just a symptom but a contributory factor to this process.

These themes of emptiness and the disappearance of the animal not only describe a sense of loss in modernity but reinforce this loss by the very terms of the analysis. In an indirect way this is reminiscent of the ambivalence so often evident in attitudes to animals, which oscillate, in varying degrees, between veneration and exploitation.[15] This ambivalence is expressed at one level by the characterization of the animal as a protean image, an object without resistance, but it also works through a voiding, intentionally or otherwise, of the significance of the animal object. The disengagement from the animal, its reduction to pure sign, *reinforces* at a conceptual level the effacement of the animal that is perceived to have taken place in reality even whilst criticizing that process. This is rather like the act of mourning as outlined by Freud:

> Just as mourning impels the ego to give up the object by declaring the object to be dead and offering the ego the inducement of continuing to live, so does each single struggle of ambivalence loosen the fixation of the ego to the object by disparaging it, denigrating it and even as it were killing it . . . Of the three preconditions of melancholia – loss of the object, ambivalence, and regression of libido into the ego – the first two are also found in the obsessional self-reproaches arising

after a death has occurred. In those cases it is unques-
tionably the ambivalence which is the motive force of
the conflict.[16]

The process of untangling oneself from the object by deni-
gration in order to help one deal with its loss appears to me to
be similarly achieved by inflating and extending the possible
meanings of the idea of the animal to the point that it
becomes almost meaningless as a concept. These theories of
loss, as a version of mourning, in fact turn out to be another
version of the flight from the animal.

In contrast to this, I propose that the representation of
animals in film generally presents a much richer and more
varied source of cultural material than the critics of modernity have appreciated. There are two dimensions to this. The
first relates to the fact that the kinds of roles that animals
often play, particularly in fiction films, involve notions of
agency and in that sense the animal, even if unintentionally,
comes to determine its effects as much as they are determined by the position it is placed in by humans. Second,
animal imagery cannot be subsumed under a general and
abstract theory of semiotics, as if the animal is a sign easily
interchangeable with other kinds of sign, because for historical reasons the visual animal carries specific connotations
particularly in relation to questions of treatment and welfare.
This factor, as we shall see, constantly erodes the boundary
between fiction and reality. Let us consider first what it means
for an animal to act.

'Animal agency' is a phrase that always needs to be qualified by the lack of power animals have in relation to that which humans have over them. However, it does redress an imbalance in the theorizing of human–animal relations by seeking, instead, to outline the impact animals have on humans rather than always seeing animals as the passive partner, or victim. In taking such a perspective I am making no assumptions about what specifically constitutes animal subjectivity or interiority, nor that there is necessarily a sense that the animal wills any specific change on human beings. Agency is defined here 'not as some innate or static thing which an organism always possesses, but rather in a relational sense which sees agency emerging as an effect generated and performed in configurations of different materials . . . anything can potentially have the power to act, whether human or non-human'.[17] The animal body is caught up, therefore, in a complicated system of reactions and effects which is registered as a play between the surfaces of bodies, but not necessarily as revealing anything about the interaction of minds. Film reflects this by not making the implied mutual alienation, consequent on the inability of animals to *speak* to humans, central to its configuration of human–animal relations and their histories. In fact, although there are plenty of *rhetorical* animals on screen – animals as metaphors, metonyms, textual creatures to be read like words, even animals that speak – much of the power of the film animal derives from the fact that in film human–animal relations are possible through the play of agency regardless of the nature of animal interiority, subjectivity or communication.

The definition of agency quoted above, invoked (ironically) under the heading of 'Actor Network Theory', seems to me to play on the ambiguity that acting is both a form of agency and something done under the direction of somebody else. In fact, if one is to consider what it means for an animal *to act* then one has to take into account not just the mechanics of training, but the whole network of interactions between animal and humans including the general effects sought by the filmmakers and their impact on an audience. To take a famous example, when Lassie climbs out of a river and, instead of doing what comes naturally to a dog, which is to shake off the water, he staggers about bedraggled and exhausted, this is seen as a mark of what makes Lassie such a great actor. Lassie is in fact doing all sorts of things: responding to his training; utilizing his understanding of the context in which he is placed; and, in a sense, behaving more like a human than a dog. Indeed, filmmaking of this kind using animals is only possible because the mutual gaze between human and animal is at some level comprehensible for both parties. Furthermore, the dog's understanding of the human expectations placed upon him/her could be said to come across on screen as the reverse of this, in the sense that here the dog engages, or manipulates, a human emotional response to its movements which now appears natural. It is in the context of these unintended effects by the animal itself that we might best understand what it means to talk about the manner in which the animal, *pace* Lippit, does regulate its symbolic effects.

One of the many chimpanzees used as Cheetah in the Tarzan films.

The second important feature to consider, which concerns the cultural connotations an animal carries in the visual field, is best analysed historically. Critics of modernity's treatment of animals, whether approaching from a postmodern perspective or not, are prone to simplify the historical trajectories of human–animal relations, particularly in their clumsy characterization of the nineteenth

Leo, the MGM mascot, and Greta Garbo, 1925.

Lassie and Elizabeth Taylor in *Lassie Come Home* (1943).

century as somehow archaic and incapable of registering the complex significations of the animal. In fact, the linkage of vision and ethics around the animal with which film engages is a significant consequence of the humanitarianism of the nineteenth century. To understand how film is locked into this issue of ethics, as it extends and transforms the visual field from the 1890s onwards, it is necessary to understand the visual status of the animal as it developed in the years leading up to the beginnings of cinema. Hilda Kean is one of the few historians who has made the connection between imagery and changes in the social status of animals. In her book *Animal Rights*, she shows not only how the actual sight of animal cruelty in the city streets gave impetus to animal welfare reform but, more significantly, she links it to the general project of social improvement and, above all, *modernization*. Thus, the development in animal welfare was not simply a sentimental or nostalgic project to recover a lost harmonious relation with the natural world, broken by industrialism and increasing urbanization, but also something forward-looking, an integral component of an improved future. The passage to modernity was, in part, defined by the treatment of animals. She writes: 'The changes that would take place in the treatment of animals relied not merely on philosophical, religious or political stances but the way in which animals were literally and metaphorically seen. The very act of seeing became crucial in the formation of the modern person.'[18] To which I would add: and in the formation the modern animal.

This important thesis has a number of important implications. The first is that humane behaviour is not simply a matter of deeds but is also a matter of being *seen* to behave humanely. By extension, the mark of a more civilized society – a common trope of animal welfare literature generally – is the way in which a society *displays* its humanity. The appearance and treatment of the animal body become a barometer for the moral health of the nation. Second, the importance of the visual is not limited simply to the relationship between the observer and the observed. That which is not seen is equally important and is also heavily codified. As Peter de Bolla writes, in relation to the Enlightenment though the point is very pertinent to this context, 'visuality is . . . the name we might give to a figurative spacing that opens up, controls, or legislates the terrain upon which a large number of contexts are articulated. In this sense visuality is certainly not confined to the visible.'[19] In the nineteenth century a concern about what should and should not be seen led to changing alignments of what was acceptable and new constructions of visual taboos. This was formally expressed through legal codes that reflected the increasing power of animal welfare sentiments and which brought human–animal relations under greater control, particularly in urban environments.

The numerous bills and acts throughout the nineteenth century that sought to regulate the treatment of animals in public places also determined what was appropriate and inappropriate for the public to see. In 1857 a Bill to

Amend the Acts for the More Effectual Prevention of Cruelty to Animals included a clause proposing that children under fourteen should not witness killing in a slaughterhouse. The quality of the physical appearance of animals on the streets was also an object of concern and the same bill recommended that strays, or dogs in an emaciated or starving state, should be destroyed. In the 1876 Act to Amend the Law Relating to Cruelty to Animals, which was largely concerned with vivisection, restrictions were placed on educational lectures in medical schools and colleges that might involve experiments as part of a demonstration. Public lectures involving such experiments were banned. In a further amending act of 1911 not only were children under sixteen forbidden to see the cutting up of carcasses, but this issue of witness was extended to the animals themselves: 'No animal shall be killed in the sight of any other animal awaiting slaughter.'[20] This last point, which extended consideration to what animals themselves see, is highly significant. Admittedly, any humanitarian aspect to this act is tempered by the fact that the animals are still being killed. Nevertheless, it does establish the idea that at some level animals are participant observers in visual culture, something that would be of key significance in film.

The distinction between appropriate and inappropriate seeing also meant that the visual appearance or image of the animal became a highly significant factor in discourses, and conflicts, over the status of the animal. However, this did not mean that the inhumane and the humane could be mapped in a straightforward way onto whether animals were visible or not. There were, and are, certain forms of public visibility that may be seen as inhumane by some and not by others: zoos, circuses and certain animal sports, for instance. In any case we can never assume a uniformity of response to what was seen in public.[21] Nevertheless, the fact that the legislation places so much emphasis on seeing gives the animal, potentially at any rate, a significant normative dimension in the visual public domain. These principles would in due course be applied to film itself with the Cinematograph (Animals) Act of 1937, which specifically addressed the issue of cruelty in filmmaking and which I shall describe in chapter two.

Legislating for the field of public vision does not entail particular consideration for the interiority of the seeing subject. What is of significance is what is measurable: surfaces, actions, events. This again relates to how the animal is seen in film, where issues of subjectivity are usually secondary to issues of agency. However, if some of the responses to animals on screen are informed by these public codes of seeing, how do these codes relate to other types of seeing, such as the shared look between human and animal individuals which is so often made the site of mutual incomprehension or alienation? In other words, how do we evaluate the extent to which the look between human and animal is informed by the moral connotations of the animal in the public domain? The animal's eye is a very significant motif in films and we need to ask what it is that film invokes by delineating this type of contact. The very fact of screening the mutual gaze between

The eye of the bison from Bill Viola's *I Do Not Know What it is I Am Like* (1986).

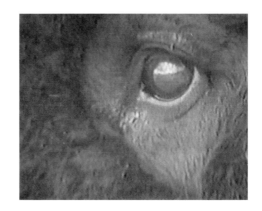

human and animal to an audience means that film is always going to play on a number of different registers that relate to both psychological and social aspects of visual contact. This effectively means that this exchange of looks is not just a form of psychic connection but also determines the practical interaction that is taking place. In that sense the exchange of the look is, in the absence of the possibility of language, the basis of a social contract.

To examine the visual construction of animals in film is to consider the animal as a visual image in a network of cultural and social associations. It is also important to consider animal representation in film within a historical perspective in order to make film part of the story of the changing status of the animal from the early nineteenth century onwards. This is particularly so in relation to the history of the institutionalization of humane sentiments through the creation of societies like the RSPCA and laws concerning animals. This changing status is very influenced by developing ideas about appropriate and inappropriate seeing as I have indicated. The implication of this framework is that it focuses less on the direct symbolic significance of the visual animal and more on its actions and effects. That these effects can be strikingly immediate or direct on audiences does not mean that the responses are any less, at some level, constructed through this historical process. A further aspect to this public dimension of seeing concerns the implications of interpreting the look of the animal. Many writers have tended to assume that the exchange of mutually incomprehensible looks between human and animal is a symptom of their alienation, though this interpretation seems to me to stem largely from an unspoken expectation that the look ought to *say* something particular. Film tends to suggest that the look is a different kind of contact, one determined by the particular nature and constraints of human–animal relations. The look need not necessarily communicate anything as such but sets in play a chain of effects that reflects at the very least some form of shared understanding of context between human and animal. However, there is a tension in this perspective. Whilst film often depicts the reinforcement of the bonds between human and animal, it also multiplies the different ways of seeing the animal, which is a mode of fragmentation too. Indeed, in many critics' accounts of the animal gaze it is the theme of fragmentation that dominates over the theme of bonding. In fact, as we shall see, it makes more sense to see them as necessarily interdependent. The multiple ways of seeing and filming the animal is rather a measure of the extent and intensity of film's engagement with the animal world.

The degree to which humans and animals are alienated from each other is sometimes gauged by the extent to which some form of mutual communication is or is not possible. This is an echo of the commonplace that it is the capacity for language that marks the difference between human and animal. Communication by the look, however, has a different set of implications because it can be seen to be more primal and perhaps also telepathic. Yet, just as some writers consider that our look towards the animal can only ever be narcissistic, so others consider it impossible to interpret the look of the animal back at us. John Berger's formulation takes the idea of mutual alienation further. In his analysis of the gaze in the zoo, neither animal nor human can centre their attention or look on each other: 'You are looking at something that has been rendered absolutely marginal; and all the concentration you can muster will never be enough to centralize it.'[22] Another version of this can be found in Catherine Russell's remarks on the animal gaze as explored in Bill Viola's video-film *I Do Not Know What It Is I Am Like* (1986): 'they look without seeing. We cannot know what they are thinking, if they are thinking; the eye becomes a mask.'[23] There is no presumption here that the look of an animal might be an active one and there is an interesting slippage in the above quote from not having access to their thinking to the absence of thinking. There is also something paradoxical in these kinds of formulations in that the otherness of the animal gaze is noted and yet described in terms of a lack in relation to the human. The eye, taken out of its context, is expected to speak.[24] Or, to put it another way, we might ask ourselves what kind of gaze do we want the animal to look back at us with?

This sense of alienation, or fragmentation, is further accentuated in the idea that the animal is objectified, or calibrated, through a surplus of different kinds of gaze, human this time. For instance, Catherine Russell, in her book on experimental and ethnographic film, describes the zoo gaze thus: 'the exoticism of animals lies *somewhere* between the excitement of the sexual spectacle and the otherness of the ethnographic subject. The zoo is an intermediary zone that lies between the pornographic and the ethnographic gazes, in a triangular relation with them.'[25] This version of the zoo gaze does not have any qualities specific to looking at animals but is derived from those gazes that most emphasize the elements of desire, voyeurism and power over other human beings. Whether this translates easily into the idea that we might describe such visual power over animals in similar terms is not quite as straightforward as it might first appear. To illustrate this we can take as an example the framing of human–animal looking in pornographic terms, which, by extension, suggests a deviant vision underlying the filming of animals. The latter combines the voyeurism noted above with motifs of wildness and violence which, in turn, associates the act of seeing with extreme manifestations of desire. Derek Bousé notes that Muybridge arranged for the killing of a buffalo in 1884 for his photographic project and describes this as a founding moment in the desire for kill scenes which 'have remained wildlife films' chief guarantor of authenticity, just as the obligatory "cum-shot" has in XXX-rated adult films.'[26] This echoes the language of Linda Williams's thesis that the beginnings of cinema represent an interpenetration of the perverse and the scientific, via the desire to look at bodies in motion ('the frenzy of the visible'). Her thesis similarly begins with Muybridge, in this instance his sequences of naked women in motion.[27]

If the history of the depiction of animals in film is over-shadowed by perverse seeing, then the logical conclusion would be that the image of the violent animal body is desired in the same way as the sexualized human body. However, the issue here is not whether similar desires might be aroused in audiences from seeing animal and human bodies in similar contexts, but what it means to map the one onto the other. At one level, the invocation of taboo imagery points to comparable ethical questions that relate to issues of exploitation – particularly where scenes of animal violence are contrived for the camera – or to the ambivalence of the interplay between extreme objectification and the thrills of identification. The parallel with pornography does have some significance at the point of action because, however contrived the context, there is no dividing line between the simulated and real for animal conflict or other forms of violence such as hunting.[28] A similar ambiguity concerning simulation can also be found in pornography, but the consequences for the animal body in the depiction of violence is much more extreme than that for the human body in the depiction of sexuality. It is this more extreme collapse between the figural and the real that makes the animal a particular type of film subject and one that is different from the human. Various conclusions can be drawn from this. If the kinds of gazes invoked to describe the manner by which the visual animal is constructed – ethnographic, pornographic – are inadequate because they derive from specific modes of depicting the human subject, then there needs to be a more specific description for the construction of the visual animal, one that takes better account of the particular positionings of the animal in relation to the human. This is especially true if we are to take into consideration one of the most interesting implications of Berger's thesis, which is that the visual is historically constitutive of human–animal relations. It is, according to Berger, 'that look between animal and man, which may have played a crucial role in the development of human society, and with which, in any case, man had always lived until less than a century ago'.[29] It is also the case that if the symbolic animal in film constantly points beyond itself to outside the frame of the screen then it cannot be characterized as dissolving into an empty or infinitely protean sign.

Although Berger's thesis is critical of modernity, the idea that the moral and political aspects of human-animal relations can be reconstructed through the visual is itself a modern outlook, even though it might be invoked as a form of primal relationship. In the broad survey of animal life that makes up the BBC's famous documentary series *Life on Earth*, first broadcast in 1979, the one moment in the series in which David Attenborough engages with animals in a direct manner, in this case gorillas, he remarks, 'there is more meaning and mutual understanding in exchanging a glance with a gorilla than any other animal I know . . . We see the world the same way that they do . . . If ever there was a possibility of escaping the human condition and living imaginatively in another creature's world it must be with that of the gorilla.' It could easily be argued that this is merely an anthropomorphic projection on Attenborough's part, standing out as it

The bird's outlook: the photographer Doug Allan with a burrowing owl chick, South Dakota.

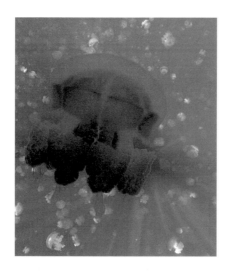

A different kind of nature documentary, Dorothy Cross's film *Come Into the Garden Maude*, (2001), which provides a meditative contemplation on jellyfish without commentary.

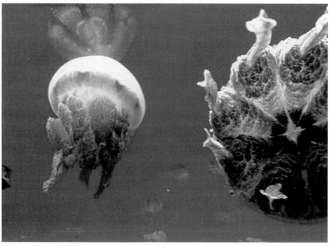

does in the context of a spectacular filmic vision of the world's wildlife achieved with great technical ingenuity. But there is another level of reading this, which we will come across in other examples, and this concerns the way in which film uses the visual to suggest that it is this seeing that actually integrates us with the natural world. In the large scale Attenborough documentaries, for instance *The Living Planet* (1991) or *State of the Planet* (2000), one is faced with a montage of different creatures and their surroundings, necessarily filmed using very different techniques. In contrast to this sometimes disparate visual array, the pulling together of these different images into a narrative that makes sense for its intended audience is underpinned by the basic idea that the interconnections are, in nature, fragile. The moral message of these films is implicit in the way in which the images of animals and environment are tied together and in the way that, as witnesses, we too become co-opted within this depiction of nature. There is a self-reinforcing cycle at work here. The act of linking the images creates the vulnerable networks that will be best served by us looking at them in appreciation rather than acting upon them detrimentally. Despite the significance of film technology in constructing these images, the shared glance with the gorilla suggests that we are looking from within nature and not at nature. Thus, rather than seeing nature films of this kind as a replacement for reality, they seem more like the point of entry for our engagement with the natural world: an active moral gaze made possible, even structured, by the technology of modernity. The question is, does such a gaze *do* anything more than simply look? In other words, is the audience that is configured by this view of the natural world any more than a consumer of this imagery or can the implicit moral message of such films create the conditions for a more positive engagement with the natural world?

The idea that film is a form of passive consumption has played an important part in debates concerning the tension between the aestheticization of nature and the political and practical aspects of animal welfare or environmental action. Answers to some of these issues are limited by the current lack of research into the reception and effects of animal film imagery in the public domain, though the natural history film industry is constantly redefining what it sees as public taste. In other words, against the background of competing ideas of audience expectation producers create programmes based on an idea of what an audience wants which then in turn appear to define public taste.[30] For instance, in the 1990s there was an increase in violence being used to sell natural history films, especially in the United States, though it is not clear whether there were any similar cultural shifts in attitudes to animals in other areas of public life.[31] At a large-scale commercial level, rifts within the construction of nature imagery are even more marked as David Ingram reveals in his discussion of Walt Disney films in relation to the formation of two environmental advocacy organizations in Hollywood in the late 1980s, the Earth Communications Office and the Environmental Media Association (EMA).[32] Disney's involvement in the EMA at the beginning of the '90s pointed up a sharp contradiction between its pro-environmental rhetoric and other, less environmentally acceptable, aspects of its business practice and depiction of nature on film. In summarizing *The Lion King* (1994) Ingram writes, 'nature in *The Lion King* is similarly an economy in which those at the top of the food chain (lions humanized as middle-class Americans) are justified in their right to consume a nature which is guaranteed to remain endlessly renewing and abundant, as long as their power and authority is not usurped by their undeserving enemies, suitably marked as inferiors in terms of class and ethnicity.'[33] Incidentally, in 1994 the film was the biggest earner in the United States, taking $298.9 million dollars at the box office.[34]

The sense of incoherence, or contradiction, that emerges from an analysis of the politics of animal film imagery takes a particular form, which relates to the cultural ambivalence noted earlier. In the case of *The Lion King* the positive, or celebratory ecological messages in the film are

Filming albatross for the Walt Disney film *Islands of the Sea* (1960).

countered by the kinds of ideological readings that are noted above. If these images of nature depicted in film mirror wider social or political relations, they also mirror the rifts within such relations. Equally important, they also reflect the structures that produced them in the first place. In the case of nature documentaries for instance, 'the natural history film-making that results is now as much about television as it is about natural history. And the practices of natural history filmmaking are now concerned with the new environments of television efficiency and accountability.'[35] So the question concerning the effects of animal film imagery on public attitudes to animals, and whether it acts as a substitution for or distraction from the actual experience of animal life, needs also to consider the fragmentary and even *ad hoc* processes that construct such imagery. In fact, these factors have an important impact on the composite nature of so much animal film and extend to film's own exploration of degrees of bonding and alienation between human and animal. In all these instances it is not possible to separate out the direct forms of contact in such bonding and the technological means by which such bonding is represented.

In Bill Viola's own comments on his video-film *I Do Not Know What It Is I Am Like* (1986), a film made up of a series of separate and stylistically different meditations on the themes of animals, humans and religious ceremony, he notes that in looking into the eye of the animal we see both the reflection of ourselves and the 'irreconcilable otherness of an intelligence ordered around a world we can share in body but not in mind.'[36] He articulates this thought in the film with a striking sequence of a slow zoom onto the eye of an owl to reveal, at extreme close-up, the reflection of Viola's own image behind his camera and tripod. The structure of Viola's film is fragmentary but it does not calibrate the animal as the sum total of combined voyeuristic gazes (pornographic/erotic, ethnographic). Rather it produces a sequence of parallel versions of looking, none of which is quite the same. The film feels, in its elements, like a collage of the main strands of animal filmmaking. For instance, it includes ethnographic elements in the depiction of a fire-walking ritual from Fiji; alludes to the early travelogues which themselves provided much animal footage; comedy in the trickery by which Viola is suddenly replaced by an elephant; time-lapse sequences of a decaying fish carcass, reminiscent of a quasi-scientific novelty first exploited before the First World War; speeded-up flashing imagery of a running dog that echoes the jerky camera work of early attempts to track animals moving at speed; and documentary in the meditative shots that focus on the extraordinary peculiarities of the bodies of birds and other creatures. There is no unifying system to this compilation except insofar as the three 'intelligences' depicted in the film – those of animals, Viola himself, and the people at the religious festival – are linked negatively via the notion of irreconcilability and impenetrability. Rather than seeing different gazes coming together around the figure of the animal, we witness instead their dispersal.

A film that raises similar issues, though in a different format, is Frederick Wiseman's *Zoo* (1993). In this documentary without commentary the camera wanders around Miami Zoo interspersing episodes in the daily life of the zoo staff with a meandering look at animals and humans alike. This is not a film in which you see much of the repetitive pacing so common to captive animals, and many of the enclosures are lush and spacious. In fact, the camera often lingers on a beautiful bird or animal just as a spectator might and the sudden clarity of a spectator's voice can disappear again in a general hubbub of human and animal sounds. At one level the film is concerned with the juxtaposition of animals, humans and events that seem somewhat arbitrarily put together. Above all, in its depiction of everything from medical operations, autopsies, wild animal dealing, feeding time, shots of children playing, trained elephants doing formation parades, to people watching animals, the film richly represents the complexity of the zoo as an institution. At the same time the depiction of animals being filmed is a significant thread that runs throughout, exemplified by an episode in which a number of different camera crews film an anaesthetized gorilla having a medical and dental check-up, whilst themselves being filmed by Wiseman. In the space of the zoo the camera appears to be as important as the naked eye. Here again we are presented with a juxtaposition of different visual genres: news, science, popular entertainment and welfare.

Finally, in outlining the different kinds of gaze, or look,

in human–animal relations it is important to consider the numerous ways in which filmmakers explore the idea of the animal gaze. For Jules-Etienne Marey, one of the first scientists to exploit sequential photography in the 1880s, the promise of the moving camera was its ability to reveal in nature what the human eye could not see. The fantasy of looking through the camera as if through the eye of an animal to reveal further those realms of nature invisible to the human eye is an extension of this idea.[37] At a more technical level, the very act of making a film using trained animals is premised on some form of mutual intelligibility in the look between human and animal. Alongside the lines of sight that link director, technicians, camera and actors are also those that link trainer to animal. In fact, trainers are often dressed up as extras on set or concealed within it so they can direct the animal's attention via auditory or visual cues. In Steve Barron's comedy *Rat* (2001), which opens with the camera scurrying rat-like around the house, the character Hubert, on his return to human form having mysteriously turned into a rat, is asked what it was like. The advantages, he claimed, were being able to see in the dark whilst, on the other hand, he did not like the way humans looked at him as if they were swallowing lemons. Seeing and being looked at are, in this film, crucial to what it feels like for a human to be a rat. Indeed, it is only Hubert as rat that can see the corrupting influence of the journalist who has moved into the family house under the pretence of writing a book on the family's experiences. In fact, the book turns out to be a description of their greedy desire to exploit Hubert's transfor-

mation whilst at the same time expressing murderous inten-
tions towards the rat. The film's happy ending, in which the
journalist is revealed for what he is and expelled from the
household, could be described as a victory for what is seen over
what is said.

One of the most significant ways in which film explores
the animal look is when that look merges with the look of the
camera lens. By fetishizing the eye – and often it is the single
eye rather than the pair – film effectively turns the animal into
a camera, a non-human recording mechanism. *The Horse
Whisperer* (Redford, 1998) is a convenient example to illustrate
this, in part because its symbolism is somewhat heavy-handed.
A horrific accident leaves a horse, Pilgrim, badly injured and
traumatized; his young rider, Grace, loses a leg. The horse is
taken across America to Montana to be treated by a man, Tom
Booker, known as a 'horse whisperer'. The film has a number of
plot motifs familiar to many animal films, such as overcoming
loss, family difficulties, and a reintegration of identity.
However, the central link between horse and human throughout the film is the look as exemplified by the frequent shots of
the horse's eye. At the beginning of the film, just before the
fateful ride, Grace asks Pilgrim, as the camera focuses on the
eye of the horse, 'What are you thinking, huh? What are you
thinking, boy?' The answer to this question, which in a sense
frames the film, given that so much depends on what the horse
thinks, can only be determined by the horse's actions.
However, it is further symbolized by the slow healing of a large
scar on the right hand side of the horse's face; the side, inci-

dentally, on which the eye is usually shown in close-up. There are several moments in the film that appear to depict the horse's vision. Once, after the accident, in which things are very blurred; then as part of a sequence of shots which track from Grace and her mother embracing, to an image of the horse's eye, to a blurred image of Tom Booker; and finally a view of the girl, slightly out of focus but luminescent. In keeping with the religious symbolism of the film, Grace is not merely visible to Pilgrim but actually illuminated as if she were a vision. In the film one sees through the perspectives of camera and animal, but not through the eyes of the human.

Pilgrim and Grace, from Robert Redford's film *The Horse Whisperer* (1998).

Despite the quasi-spiritual overtones implied by the myth of horse-whispering, the film portrays no magical way of speaking to the animal beyond the look and the touch, patient therapeutic procedures with the horse which require the passage of time. Indeed, the film consigns horse-whispering to voiceover: '[horses] first came to know man as the hunted knows the hunter . . . For the fear he struck in their hearts was too deep to be dislodged. Since that Neolithic moment when a horse was first haltered there were those among men who understood this. They could see into a creature's soul and soothe the wounds they found there. The secrets uttered softly into troubled ears. These men were known as the whisperers.' However, Tom Booker is not a mythic figure. Rather, the domain he occupies is governed by the look, which determines all the significant gestures and bodily attitudes that are required for some sort of rapprochement between human and animal.

The Horse Whisperer's conclusion, when Grace finally manages to ride Pilgrim again, means that the trauma is overcome even if we cannot assume that the different lines of sight are necessarily united. The cure is judged by outer signs. Indeed, as in numerous films interweaving human and animal themes, the look that marks the point of contact across the species is not itself demystified. It is still a point of resistance but one that does not entail a radical alienation between human and animal. This may seem surprising given that many of these films play so much on themes of anthropomorphism and sentimentality, but such ambiguities run throughout the depiction of human–animal relations. The horse itself is something of a double figure. In Hintz's book *Horses in the Movies*, he notes that horses occupy an important place, particularly for younger viewers, because they are both powerful and yet easily domesticated, taking up the virtual status of a pet. (Though he notes that the affection of horse for man is greatly exaggerated in movies.)[38] Horses are not like dogs yet fulfil a more satisfying sense of mastery. In the case of *The Horse Whisperer* the overcoming of the trauma enables the horse to be controlled again by his owner. But although human mastery is reestablished at the end of the film it is proved to be fragile through the interlinking of the fates of horse and rider.

A much darker version of the traumatic encounter of human and horse is found in the film *Equus* (Lumet, 1977), based on Peter Shaffer's play of the same name, in which a boy undergoes psychiatric treatment for blinding six horses. The plot of the film follows the investigations of the psychiatrist, Martin Dysart, to understand the causes of this mutilation and ends with the boy confessing, or rather re-enacting, his crime. Again, this is a film that plays a great deal on the gaze of the horse and on eyes generally. The boy, Alan, has deified the horse and he comes to see the look of the horse that so traumatizes him as, ultimately, a look of judgement. Alan worships and eroticizes his horse–god, Equus, and develops his own private religious ritual by taking a horse out at night, intoning special phrases and riding the horse naked. In his mind he becomes one with it.[39] The crisis which leads to the blinding of the horses occurs when, in the stable, he finds himself unable to make love to the stable girl, Jill, because of the judgmental image of the horse–god's look. He imagines Equus mocking his inadequacy and observing everything he does, which leads him to start stabbing the horses: 'Equus . . . noble Equus . . . faithful and true . . . godslave . . . thou god . . . seest . . . nothing.'

The act of blinding breaks Alan's identification with the horse though he only returns to what the psychiatrist identifies as 'normality' when he re-enacts the blinding in a therapy session at the end of the film. However, during the film the psychiatrist comes to envy Alan's primal worship in the light of his own repressed life. Both the father figures in the film – Alan's father, who goes to pornographic movies, and the psychiatrist, who has a sexless marriage – are similarly emasculated; an ambiguity reflected in the figure of the horse as both master and mastered. As Dysart says at the beginning, 'I'm wearing that horse's head myself. That's the feeling. All reined up in old language and old assumptions, straining to jump clean-hoofed on to a whole new track of being I only suspect is there. I can't see it . . . the only thing I know for sure is this: a horse's head is unknowable to me.' At the end of the film, with the promise of Alan's cure, it will be the psychiatrist who will in turn become haunted by Equus and by the look of the horse that he reads as one that says 'Account for me.' The fundamental unknowability of the horse problematizes all the links in the film: between God and animal, disturbed child and animal, father and son, doctor and patient, and so on. These links and patterns of identification are not

Ritual horse worship in Sidney Lumet's film *Equus* (1977).

The blinding of the horses from *Equus* (1977).

Equus eye.

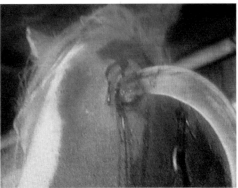

submerged in any way but their difficulty is realized by the look of the horse, which effectively collapses the idea of the superego (God, the father, the lawmaker) into the animal body. Indeed, whereas earlier in the film Dysart sees Equus looking back at him, by the end he is truly in the dark, striking out in his imagination with a pick just as Alan had done.

Slavoj Zizek makes the point, in his brief remarks on *Equus* (though on the play rather than the film), that the plot replays the lie that myth is somehow separate from, or an alternative to, modernity rather being integral to it. Myth is inserted in the past by modernity itself: 'as is well known the celebration of the return of barbaric mythopoeic violence in the process of modernization was one of the main themes of conservative modernism in the arts.'[40] Thus, it could be argued that what appear to be versions of archaic myths and figures, like the horse–god and the act of sacrifice, are in fact integral to the construction of modernity. In addition, an important point in *Equus* is the fact that neither parentage nor religious teaching nor even myths can explain the arbitrariness of why a boy might worship a horse as a god. To this arbitrariness must be added the fact that modernity's need for myth as a justification for its own inherent and returning barbarism is a precarious and unstable one. In the move from play to film the mythic, symbolic aspects of the animal are stripped out and we get much closer to the strangeness of the literal conjunction of horse and boy. This was something for which the film was criticized. By contrast, in the original stage play, premiered in 1973, the drama was conceived along classical lines with the cast on stage, surrounding the main set, for the entire play and some tiered seating behind for some of the audience 'in the fashion of a dissecting theatre'.[41] The actors playing the horses had masks, through which their heads were clearly visible and were instructed that 'any literalism which could suggest the cosy familiarity of a domestic animal – or worse, a pantomime horse – should be avoided . . . Animal effect must be created entirely mimetically.' The masks needed to be put on before the audience with precise timing for an 'exact and ceremonial effect'.[42] In the film the blinding is also graphically re-enacted. Although Alan lunges about wildly with a sickle the shift to the close-up shots of the penetration of the eye show a precise aim. Whilst this act does finally resolve something for Alan, the problem of the gaze of the horse, and indeed the mind of the horse, is transferred from patient to doctor. At least, whilst the horse still sees there is some shape to actions and events, even if the look is traumatizing. Once the horse is blinded, as Dysart comes to understand, the world becomes unknowable.

These therapeutic themes are explored through animals in a whole range of different kinds of films. Although a film like *Equus* suggests that the animal look may be ultimately unbearable, many films suggest the opposite. The paradox is that the failure to understand the look does not entail the breakdown of contact even if, as film sometimes suggests, the look is all we have. It can be a site of trauma or of healing. A benign version of this can be found in the first *Free Willy* film (1993), which, like *The Horse Whisperer*, explicitly links human and animal loss. Here, the look between the child Jesse and the whale is a sign of mutual recognition but it is also something more. The plot of the film concerns the delinquent Jesse coming to terms with his placement with foster parents. His relationship with a similarly troubled whale in the aquarium that he goes to work in, and his eventual release of the whale, parallel his acceptance of his own position as a foster child. As with *The Horse Whisperer*, the narrative tropes in these kinds of animal films are not particularly complicated and in their rite-of-passage structure the films act as moral fables. Although it is possible to provide complex and sophisticated readings of these films, their simplicity also marks them as a form of humane pedagogy or moral instruction dominated by the primacy of the visual relation.

The idea of the look as something more than simply recognition is linked to the magical elements that are found in even the most secular of fables. Randolph, an Indian who also works in the aquarium and who tells Jesse Indian myths about the whale, says that the eyes 'can look into a man's soul if they want. Willy, he won't look at Ray or me. Maybe he sees you.' The instantaneity of the look, like the snapshot, is important. Willy, the film implies, in some way *knows* that Jesse is like him, or on his side, through their exchange of looks. If a character has no means of communicating their personal narrative, the specifics of their sense of loss, then they naturally fall back on the look, the gesture and the touch. In fact, Jesse will successfully train Willy to do tricks, and ultimately set the whale free, through the use of gestures.[43] This idea of the instant contact between human and animal has both mythical and modern connotations. It taps into the old idea that it is possible to commune with animals, or that this communing is like a form of spiritual second sight, but one can also read this instantaneity as a characteristic of the modern world: 'animals were particularly useful in the development of technical media because they seemed to figure a pace of communication that was both more rapid and more efficient than that of language.'[44] Words related to rapidity and efficiency also express the language of optimization. Film fetishizes the animal look to such a degree that it could be suggested that it is around the idea of visual communication that the animal figure comes closest to resembling the technology that produces it. In other words, as Lippit indicates, it is the point at which the animal becomes most machine-like. The telepathic relation between boy and whale is suggested in the film as a product of a primal, or archetypal, form of communing with animals, but it is also a telepathy characterized and desired by the technology of modernity. One could argue, in the context of these examples, that film does seek to idealize the kinds of transparent relations and identifications between humans and animals, but it also reveals the points at which these identifications break down.

John Huston's *Moby Dick* (1956) provides a good example of how we might look at this tension between wanting to identify with the animal and the impossibility of ever truly achieving it.[45] The film itself was a complicated undertaking shot largely at sea. Three 100-foot rubberized, steel-reinforced whales were built for filming on location, whilst for studio shooting one large whale was built and twenty smaller versions for various close shots. The artificiality of the models was countered with footage of real whaling made with the help of Portuguese whalers who were, at the time, still hunting from open longboats.[46] The film raises the possibility that in the 'madness' induced by Ahab's obsessive pursuit of the whale, the identification between human and whale is a projection of disturbed fantasies. When they are realized at the end, they bring a descent into nothingness. The relationship between human and whale is underpinned by narcissism – 'the sea where each man as in a mirror finds himself' – and reinforced by Ahab's own whale-like persona. The Captain is described as a 'man torn apart from crown to heel and spliced back together again with sperm whalebone in place of what's missing', a man marked both inside and out by the whale. Ahab's obsession with the whale comes to infect the whole crew to the point that Starbuck, the sceptical chief officer, no longer recognizes his crew as they fall under Ahab's spell. Indeed the crew doubt their own eyes when sighting the white whale: 'Aye, we all see it, but that doesn't mean it's real necessarily.' An interesting conjunction of ideas arises here because what lies beneath the sea, the faces of the men, even the whale itself appear at one level to be more important than what is on the surface. As Ahab says, 'all visible objects are but as pasteboard masks . . . [the white whale] is but a mask. It is the thing behind the mask I chiefly hate. The malignant thing that has plagued and frightened men since time began.'[47] Yet, what

John Huston (right) in the mouth of the whale during the filming of *Moby Dick* (1956).

One of the many whale models for *Moby Dick*.

really occurs in the film can only be, as the mirror imagery and the symmetries between Ahab and Moby Dick indicate, a play between visible surfaces. Doubts or questions in relation to what the whale is, or what motivates the whaling crew, all become irrelevant once the whale breaks the surface and the cycle of violence is set in train. In other words, despite Ahab's remarks, this is not purely a conflict of the underneath, the need to destroy the evil other behind the mask. After all, the vision of the deep is identical to what occurs on the surface of the sea – 'look ye into the deeps and see the everlasting slaughter that goes on.' What is of significance, and what really frames the contact between human and animal, is the manner in which the whale erupts into the field of vision.[48]

The obsession with needing to see the white whale, one that is different from all other whales, means that the most visible whale is the most important whale. To catch him, Ahab needs to predict where Moby Dick will be, based on the other sightings as recorded on his charts. Ahab's eyes are open perpetually; he does not sleep. In fact, the gold coin that he nails to the mast as a reward for the first man to sight the whale – 'skin your eyes for him' – becomes another eye, the Captain's eye on the crew.[49] These motifs of seeing, which recur throughout the film, extend to Moby Dick himself. At the climax of the film, as the boats set out to kill Moby Dick, a series of shots intercut between Ahab and the whale's eye.[50] As Ahab climbs onto the whale's body the close-up on the whale's eye is a reversal of the mastery of vision. Ahab stabs futilely at the whale's body, becoming increasingly entangled in the harpoon ropes, whilst the whale looks on, before plunging down and drowning him. Ahab's ultimate fate is not to penetrate the mask but to remain tied to the surface of the whale staring outwards.

Moby Dick's concern with the limits of identification between human and animal, is physically realized in Ahab's demise. This suggests that the proliferation throughout the film of ideas of similarity between man and beast (a proliferation matched by the increasing significance of eyes – the coin, the crew, the looks exchanged between Starbuck and Ahab, the whale), is really an intensifying drive towards an impossible identification. At one level the identification between hunter and hunted is supposed to enable the passage to mastery: only by putting oneself in the place of the prey can one seek to overcome it. However, as the roles of hunter and hunted switch, so this form of identity, or mimicry, becomes

Whale's eye,
Moby Dick.

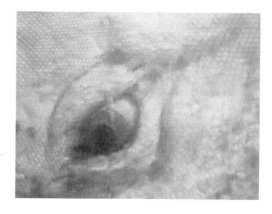

uncontrollable. This relation could be anthropomorphized through a sharing of traits of, say, love, hatred, vengeance, or even madness, yet, because the relations between Ahab and the whale are also articulated through the field of vision, the significance of these interior states is balanced by a constant sense of their limits. Ultimately, whatever the inner states might be, it is the visible interactions between the surfaces of the animal and human body that determine the nature of the relationship. In other words, identification between human and animal does not automatically imply anthropomorphism, or even its opposite, the bestialization of man.

In another, rather less successful, whale movie, *Orca – Killer Whale* (1977), many of the motifs of *Moby Dick* are replayed but with an added technological theme. The plot concerns a fisherman, Nolan, who in attempting to catch a female whale kills both her and her unborn child. The male partner whale then pursues Nolan, picking his associates off one by one (displaying particular intelligence in the destruction of the town's fuel depot) and causing enough havoc to have Nolan expelled from the fishing community. Eventually the whale leads him to his death. There are two parallel technological motifs in the film, concerning vision and communication, which relate to the patterns of identification that structure the relations between Nolan and the whale. First, the film copies the shots of the eye of the whale from *Moby Dick* as the whale tracks his prey. During one of the whale's attacks on Nolan's boat the camera focuses on the eye of the whale and, as Nolan's reflection on the surface of the orca's eye becomes clearer and clearer, like an image on a lens coming into focus, the whale effectively photographs him. This is the active gaze of the animal, which, like the camera's, fixes the individual and records him. The second theme, concerning communication, is articulated in a lecture given in the film by a scientist, who remarks on the possible superior intelligence and communication skills of the whale. Whale communication can only be understood by computer analysis and could be described as quasi-telepathic: 'What are they saying? For that matter do they have to say anything to communicate? Their sonar would be a little like our having x-ray vision.' It is not that these motifs of the camera and the sonar make the monstrous orca machine-like, for they amount to little more than minor details in the film, but they do configure that conjunction of an immediate, and transparent, natural communication on the one hand, and technology on the other. In the final part of the film the whale leads the boat and its crew further and further north to their eventual destruction. The voiceover of the scientist remarks: 'Nolan seemed to give no thought to fight or flight. The creature led, Nolan followed. If there were any other purpose to what we were doing only the orca knew it.' The suspension of will, the imitation of the animal, particularly reflected in the shifting identities of hunter and hunted, suggests that identification (mimesis) is itself a version of communication. While Nolan's following of the whale is portrayed as a form of contract between the two of them it should also be noted that the orca is to some extent anthropomorphized, but as a superhuman;

the common qualities that might make him comparable to humans – thought and language – have already been shown to be beyond reception by human senses. In this peculiar montage of themes the impossibility of contact with the whale at the level of mind and speech is compensated for by another, and to some extent agreed, link based on mutual seeing and the consequences of action. Certainly, the desire for vengeance and the challenge of conflict drive the actions of both Nolan and the orca. But the model of a transparent understanding by which this comes to be played out derives from technology (the camera, the sonar, the x-ray) and not from some primal sharing of instincts.

The image of the animal's eye reflects the *possibility* of animal understanding by emphasizing animal sight. This does not mean that the eye gives any access to what is understood but it does signal the significant participation of the animal in the visual field. What are, then, the similarities and differences between the look of the human and the look of the animal that film articulates? Sometimes film suggests that these looks mirror each other, the similarly traumatized look of Grace and Pilgrim in *The Horse Whisperer* for instance, without implying that the content of the looks is necessarily the same. The looks are parallel but not identical. Such films emphasize that the impossibility of fully understanding the animal look, or the likelihood of only seeing our own look returned to us, may not signal human alienation from the animal world. Appreciation of the asymmetry between the human and animal look may be necessary to some form of mutual recognition. In fact, the possibility that this is merely a fantasy or idealization of human–animal relations is mitigated by the fact that film also constantly exploits the limitations of seeing and plays on the disjunctions between what we see and what we know. This is why the difference of the animal look might mark the boundary between animal and human, but this boundary is also fluid. It is constantly subject both to the ambiguities of the status of the animal and the ways in which the exchange of looks keeps that boundary shifting. Whilst animals may contribute to the *shaping* of the figure of the human, that does not mean that they necessarily negatively *define* it.

The implications of this point, particularly in relation to the problem of knowing, are well illustrated by examining the role of the animal in Ridley Scott's *Blade Runner* (1982), a film that also takes up the theme of surfaces previously discussed in relation to *Moby Dick*. The film is set in the future and concerns the tracking down of a rogue group of replicants, who have returned to earth, by an expert hunter known as a blade runner. These replicants are highly developed, display emotions and are almost indistinguishable from humans. Their memories of childhood are implanted in them. A key ambiguity in the film that has been the subject of a great deal of commentary, although essentially an undecidable issue, is whether the blade runner, Deckard, played by Harrison Ford, is himself a human or not. This is understood to turn on the epistemological question of how we know with certainty what we are. However, the test to determine whether someone is human or not pivots on replies to questions, at least those asked in the film, about responses to animals. In *Blade Runner* it is the eye's response to the question of the animal that enables the difference between human and replicant to be determined. The eye betrays the status of the non-human. The apparatus used by the blade runner to test whether someone is a replicant or not is called a Voigt-Kampff Test. This measures involuntary fluctuations of the iris, capillary dilation (blush response) and changes in body chemistry when the subject answers a series of questions. The irises shown on the machines in the film were stock footage from Oxford Scientific Films.[51] The questions for the test, as asked in the film, mainly concern animals: What would you do if you came upon a tortoise on its back in a desert? What happens when you are given a calfskin wallet on your birthday? What do you do when your little boy shows you a killing jar which he uses for his butterfly collection or you have a wasp on your arm? Although the answers given in the film are intriguing – the giver of the birthday present would be reported to the police, the little boy would be taken to the doctor – from the point of view of the tester they are not of relevance by themselves. Their only significance is their relationship to the fluctuations of the eye. As Elissa Marder has pointed out, the test is ironic: 'humans can only determine their difference from the species that they have created (androids) by invoking their nostalgic empathy for the species that they have presumably already destroyed (animals).'[52] The presumption is that animals give a better indication of specifically human qualities, but ones that are measured not by cognitive reactions but by physical reflexes. Despite the ambiguities that the film presents about the status of the human as a problem of memory and consciousness, the use of the animal figure to define human difference carries the trace of the idea in which the animal negatively defines the qualities of the human.

Despite Scott Bukatman's point that there is no nature in *Blade Runner*, the film constantly invokes the idea of the natural.[53] This most industrial of environments is closer to certain conceptualizations of nature than its imagery might suggest: a multifaceted veneer covering a traditional concept of a natural order. The film, like *Moby Dick*, is a hunt movie in which the hunter is conceived, at least by implication, as being no different from his prey. Indeed, Deckard's increasing attachment to the replicant Rachel corresponds to the growing possibility that he, too, is a replicant. At the end of *Blade Runner* Deckard himself becomes the pursued. Deckard is also reminiscent of the sportsman as photographer, discussed further in chapter two: the man with both gun and lens. The lens in this case is his testing device that magnifies the eye. Hierarchy is clearly signalled by the ziggurat-shaped building that houses the Tyrell company, the manufacturer of replicants. At the bottom, on the teeming streets of the rainforest-like city, people of all races carry on their various businesses, which include the manufacture of artificial animals. (The makers of animals are depicted as Asian or Middle Eastern, a contrast to the human-replicant creator, the white Dr Tyrell.) Animals and birds play a number of roles in *Blade Runner*, and are largely totemic. Tyrell is associated with birds; Deckard dreams of a white unicorn, which implies something about the possible fantasy status of his memories; and, as Roy Batty, the leader of the renegade replicants, dies he releases the white dove he has been holding, which flies off into a very different blue sky from those seen before.[54] Replicant animals are also expensive, reflecting their exotic status. In other words, animals are singular items of fantasy, their uniqueness standing out from the teeming world of humans.[55]

Like the other films I have explored, *Blade Runner*'s persistent connection between the eye and the animal is also related to matters of surfaces and visible action, or reaction. Moreover, the replicants' responses to the animal questions in the test are more than simply affective, given that they refer to the institutions that formally govern human–animal relations. Interactions with animals are legally regulated, hence Rachel's replies that she will call in the legal authorities in relation to the birthday present of the calfskin wallet or the medical authority to stop the boy killing butterflies. In this way questions of epistemological doubt brought on by a changing technology sit curiously at odds with outmoded animal welfare sentiments in a world in which real animals no longer appear to exist; artificial animals are totems and hunters have guns. Critics have focused on the dream figure of the unicorn as the deciding factor as to whether Deckard is a replicant or not; but as Ridley Scott has commented, 'they've actually missed the wider issue. It is not the unicorn itself which is important but the green landscape around it critics should be noticing.'[56] Although Scott's remark relates to the natural landscape that has been lost, it also points towards that pastoral version of pre-industrialized nature that the scenery of the film covers over, but which returns constantly in translated forms.

If the artificial animals in *Blade Runner* are built on similar lines to the humans and bleed as the replicants do when damaged, then the film offers an intriguing take on the animal as machine. It offers a model that is much closer to the idea of the cloned organic animal than to the mechanistic animal envisaged by animatronics, which I shall discuss in the next chapter. In *Blade Runner* the animals have totemic and mythic roles while also being both organic and technological; they are biological machines. This combination means that they cannot be described purely as objects of nostalgia or as symbols of a vanished 'natural' past, without, at the same time, considering their futuristic nature and vice versa. These two aspects coincide in modernity's treatment of the animal and, if anything, point towards the ambivalent status the animal has in relation to the passage of history. Their mythic status points to something timeless while their modernity is established by their relationship to technology. *Blade Runner*'s aesthetic also combines the hi-tech and the old-fashioned – 'a film set forty years hence, made in the style of forty years ago' – which adds a further layer of historical indeterminacy to the film.[57] Even the tragic structure of the film – most of the characters are doomed to a predetermined death

– suggests a more *natural* cycle at work hidden beneath the chaos of images, temporalities and illusions.

Blade Runner simultaneously raises doubts about the reliability of visual evidence and yet seems to propose the possibility of some form of certainty via the figure of the eye. This conundrum replays a greater doubt, which concerns how film relates to reality. Stanley Cavell has argued that film itself presents a moving image of scepticism because it presents an image of reality while screening human subjectivity from the world.[58] Cavell plays on the double notion of screening as both concealing and providing. The relationship between animal figures and our ambivalent knowledges has some bearing on this idea. In *Blade Runner*, the appearance of animals is interestingly one of the few areas in which doubt is suspended. In fact, we are supposed to be certain that all the animals are to be recognized as artificial.[59] Animal artificiality is taken as read. Furthermore, the totemic creatures serve to map the human order: Roy Batty's (mechanical) dove that he releases at this death marks his (mechanical) soul; Tyrell's birds signify his panoptic and predatorial role; the fantasy of the unicorn pretty much confirms that Deckard's memories are fantasies.

However, although the non-human in the form of artificial animals mirrors the identities that appear to define human order, they also mark the point at which this order breaks down.[60] This is why the reductive characterization of the animal as a metaphor does not do justice to the full play of the diversity and significance of the animal on film. By signalling those areas in which symbolic systems also collapse, the animal figure becomes an impossible metaphor. It cannot symbolize that which is itself in flux. In Cavell's stunning reading of Howard Hawks's *Bringing up Baby* (1938), a film also described as a pursuit movie, in which the roles of hunter and hunted keep switching – 'the attempt at flight is forever transforming itself into a process of pursuit' – another (double) animal similarly marks the collapse and transformation of order. At the end of the film, when comic confusion reigns in a police station, exacerbated by the problem of two indistinguishable stray leopards, one wild and one tame, Cavell notes that the two leopards are never shown within the same frame. 'It thus acknowledges that while in this narrative fiction there are two leopards, in cinematic fact there is only one; one Baby with two natures; call them wild and tame, or call them latent and aroused. It is this knowledge, and acknowledgement, that brings a man in a trance of innocence to show his acquisition of consciousness by summoning the courage to let it collapse.'[61] In film, the animal so often presides over disorder but also in some sense shapes it towards some form of reunion or resolution, or, in the case of *Blade Runner*, loss.

Terry Gilliam's *Twelve Monkeys* (1995) also uses animals to foreground questions about looking, loss, the juxtaposition of different types of time, and a biology that is pressing at the edges and vulnerability of human existence. This film, incidentally, was also co-written by David Peoples, who contributed to the final scripting of *Blade Runner*, and the film uses a similar aesthetic, mixing the futurist with the archaic. The plot of the film concerns a man, James Cole, who is sent back in time to locate a virus and the people who released it. The consequences of the plague are described by the intertitle at the beginning of the film: five billion people will die from a deadly virus in 1997 and that the survivors will abandon the surface of the earth – 'Once again the animals will rule the world.' The film begins and climaxes with James Cole as a child seeing his adult future self shot and, like *Blade Runner*, plays in its opening phases on the seeing eye motif.[62] Animal imagery permeates all the fragmented worlds of *Twelve Monkeys*, linking the psychological and the historical themes of the film, and represents, at different points, both freedom and restriction. There are scenes of animals roaming wild and being experimented on in laboratories.[63] There is a shot of a stuffed bear in a shop window that becomes a wild bear in the post-holocaust city. A monkey is lowered down a pipe with a camera on its head holding a beef sandwich on a rescue mission. A scene is shown from Hitchcock's *The Birds*. In those scenes set in the future, Cole is sent above ground to collect insect specimens for the scientists underground – encountering a lion and a bear in the snowbound post-apocalyptic city – and, because he has no collecting bottle, eats a spider in his asylum bed at night, like the lunatic patient in *Dracula*. When Cole and his fellow fugitive Kathryn Railly are attempting to escape to the airport at the end of the film the liberated zoo animals are seen running along the freeways as if in a postmodern urban safari park.

And so on. An irony that the film exploits is that it is animal experimentation that will lead to the development of a virus that will put humans back in underground cages and set the animals free. This cyclical image is juxtaposed to the notion of time travel and the possibility that you have to go back in time to change history. The freeing of the animals from the city zoo in Philadelphia by animal activists – 'The Army of the Twelve Monkeys' – marks the beginning of the collapse of civilization and coincides with the release of the virus, thus indicating the two related trajectories of history. The first trajectory is archaic figured by the release or resurfacing of totemic bears and lions, the wild animals that benefit from the cataclysm and indicate the return of a pastoral nature at the end of history. The second trajectory is modern and concerns the intrinsic relationship of the animal to scientific invention: the movement of history through the changes brought about by, in this instance, biological experiment. The animal is effectively the linking element between these two domains, sending history backwards and forwards at the same time and crystallizing the centrality of the visual animal to modernity's contradictions.

Twelve Monkeys raises a number of questions concerning the manner in which animals attract the eye of the viewer of the film. The animals seem full of significance and yet haunt the edges of the film as ineffectually as the Army of the Twelve Monkeys, whose circular clock-like logo, spraypainted on fliers and buildings, appears to indicate to those in the future that they have changed history, whereas in fact they have not. The release of the invisible virus by a disaffected scientist and the visible release of the zoo animals by the Army both coincide at the beginning of the catastrophe that will destroy most of the human race. This construction of animals as a significant marginality in the film is best exemplified by a peripheral detail, one that gave rise to the title of a documentary on the making of the film, *The Hamster Factor* – the title is a phrase coined to refer to Gilliam's filmmaking style and his disproportionate obsession with minutiae. In one scene, as James Cole draws a sample of his own blood in a laboratory, to be tested after he has been above ground on his collecting mission, there is to the right of the shot the silhouette of a hamster on a wheel, backlit but barely noticeable within an opaque glass case. Most viewers are likely to miss this detail unless it is pointed out to them. What was intended during the shoot to be a quick take was complicated by the hamster not doing what it was supposed to do at the right time. Terry Gilliam, someone remarks in the documentary, spent that particular night more preoccupied with the hamster's performance than with that of Bruce Willis as James Cole.

There are many ways, if one is so minded, of reading the hamster on the wheel in relation to the plot motifs that concern time travel and circularity, the asylums and prisons in which Cole spends so much time, and various more marginal themes and images that concern animal experimentation and liberation. At another level the flickering silhouette of the hamster on the opaque glass is a peculiarly filmic image putting us in mind of the spool and the projector. The hamster is also a childhood pet, but one more subject to restriction than a dog or cat. In a sense the 'Hamster Factor' dramatizes the curious status of animals on film. At one level they are of considerable significance and the object of detailed attention, and yet in other ways they are often marginalized in relation to the main frame of human interest. However, what appears to be an inconstant fluctuation between the centre and margins of film is also indicative of the flexibility and omnipresence of animal imagery. What becomes crucial is not so much their status within the film's narrative as their effect: how they capture, distract or intensify our attention.

Robert Altman's detective film *The Long Good-bye* (1973) exemplifies this by playfully framing the beginning and end of the film around the motif of a missing cat, and filling the rest of the film with dogs. The long opening sequence depicts the elaborate efforts of Phillip Marlowe to feed his cat a cat food it does not like. This leads to its departure from his apartment, and it does not return for the rest of the film. At the end of the film the last spoken lines, just before Marlowe shoots his old friend Terry Lennox, whom he has finally tracked down, are, 'and I lost my cat'. Throughout the film there are numerous shots of dogs: the guard dogs at a Malibu colony, dogs wandering or lying in the road, dogs having sex in the street of a Mexican town. This example does show how easily films switch between human patterns and narratives to animal patterns and narratives as they co-exist in a quasi-dependent fashion without necessarily having much directly to do with each other. In other words, there is a curious combination of detachment and dependency. Rather than seeing animals purely as semiotic devices it makes more sense to see them as dynamic and fluid agents that are integral to passages of change. Even where it appears to be the case that animals point to a more natural or pastoral world, this is a role articulated by technology and therefore provided purely by modernity.

2 vision and ethics

The two most important themes that make the film animal significant for modernity are, first, the central place of the animal in the development of film technology and, second, the unresolvable dialectic between humane and cruel attitudes to animals that governs their history in modern culture. Animals were an important force in driving the new technology of moving film, as well as often being its inspiration. Capturing animals on film presented technological challenges, which in turn reinforced the novelty of film via the animal's own potential for novelty and its power to fascinate. This is a theme that one can trace in film history from the photographic sequences of Muybridge, Marey and Anschütz to the early films of the Lumière Brothers and others in the later 1890s, and again in the history of special effects and trick photography, from Percy Smith's juggling insects to the powerful combinations of animatronics, models and computer graphic imagery (CGI) in films such as *Jurassic Park* (1993) and television series such as the BBC's *Walking with Dinosaurs* (1999) and its recent sequel *Walking with Beasts* (2001).

The relationship between technology and questions of ethics and animal welfare is not necessarily a direct one,

Early devices for recording or simulating animal movement as illustrated in E. J. Marey's *Animal Mechanism* (1874).
Top: horses' hooves;
centre: bird flight;
botton: the wings of an insect.

Fig. 44.—This figure represents a trotting horse, furnished with the different experimental instruments; the horseman carrying the register of the pace. On the withers and the croup are instruments to show the reactions.

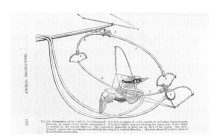

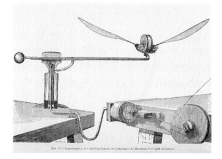

except when technical alternatives are used where animal filming might be unsafe or cause suffering to the animal. However, by constantly raising the profile of the animal body and saturating visual culture with all forms of animal imagery, film locates questions of the place of the animal in modernity at the junction where technology and issues of the treatment of animals meet.[1] In fact, the theory that the animal is becoming increasingly virtual, that its fate is to disappear into technological reproduction to become nothing more than imagery, would make sense were it not for the fact that this imagery is not uniform but unavoidably fragmented, both in terms of the technical variety of its reproduction and in terms of the various conflicts around the image itself. Just as the animal image is divided by cultural contests over its status, so the image is made up, technologically, by a process that usually depends on some form of montage. More than most other forms of filmmaking, animal cinematography invariably requires considerable editing to fit the different shots into the required narrative structures. The diverse arrays of animal size, speed of movement and accessibility mean that the techniques of recording need to change constantly, even if the final imagery is often brought into some sort of visual or temporal conformity, such as slow motion shots of flying creatures or magnification for insects, for instance. These assemblages can be somewhat arbitrary and the same stock animal footage is frequently re-used in different films serving different plotlines. Whilst this means that the images can easily be manipulated to fit various narrative fictions, particularly anthropocentric ones, they also just as easily lend themselves to counter-narratives.

The charge that animal films overplay human concerns usually derives from attending particularly to narrative frameworks and animal symbolism. Whilst this aspect of animal films is important, exclusive focus on it maintains a bias in historical writings about animals of what one might call reading the textual animal at the expense of looking at the visual animal. A good instance of these textual tropes in historical writing can be found in R. W. Jones's study of London Zoo in the nineteenth century: 'animals were to be viewed as *metonyms* of imperial triumph, civic pride, and the beneficence of God or scientific discovery', or Harriet Ritvo's examination of the 'rhetorical animals' of the Victorians.[2] This distinction reflects the fact that not enough scholarly attention has been paid to the historical study of animals in visual culture, and especially to their particular role in film, photography and painting. Perhaps this is a tacit recognition of the theoretical difficulties presented by the potential of animal visual imagery to bear a more abstract, ambivalent, relationship to the idea of the human. However, aside from the fact that film seeks to frame the animal symbolically in terms of given cultural preoccupations, film is also an extension of other practices of human–animal relations which impact on filmmaking at every level. These include the hunting techniques used to get camera shots of animals in the wild; the taming, training and bonding required when humans and animals interact on film; and the

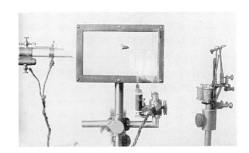

Mechanisms specifically designed to capture on film the flight of insects. Top: Lucian Bull's insect activated camera, c.1910.

Contemporary devices used by Oxford Scientific Films in the laboratory (centre) and in the wild (bottom).

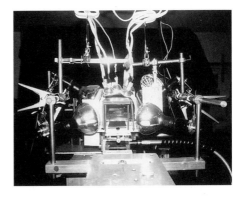

killing, whether contrived or observed in nature, that provides cinematic excitement and shock. All of these practices have important visual components, and they all imbue both the content and the processes of filmmaking. These are also practices about which modernity has become increasingly divided, although such concern can also be found from the earliest days of animal filmmaking. This I shall discuss shortly.

My interest in the wider relations of animal film imagery to modernity will link the manipulation of images by film to a more fluid social context, rather than simply focusing on issues of depiction. Furthermore, I shall take into account the fact that the variety of animal films, and the variety of roles that animals play in films generally, express the multifaceted nature of human–animal relations, which in themselves are not necessarily systematic. A nature documentary might narrate the life of a creature in anthropomorphic terms or might show a time-lapse sequence of maggots devouring a carcass, of the kind made by Oxford Scientific Films. This variety gives a complex aspect to the assessment of the relationship between the richness of animal imagery and the systems of meanings of which it is a part. In a sense, it is just as appropriate to see animal film imagery as a way of working out a mix of different factors rather than as a simple reflection of a rigid animal symbolism. An example of this mixed perspective can be found in Paul Crowson's historical account of Oxford Scientific Films, when he writes of the footage they achieved, after considerable technical difficulty,

Time-lapse sequence of the decaying body of a woodmouse by Oxford
Scientific Films.

of a brown trout laying eggs: 'The spectacle was breathtaking. Such an observation may seem to be of little practical use: it won't relieve the world's fuel shortage . . . Yet it always generates wonder and humility and so contributes to man's health and peace of mind.'[3] Here the gains are both scientific and therapeutic, as well as invoking a sense of sublimity. This ethical language – the moral and social benefits of animal films – sits at odds with the practices of destruction and upheaval that humans wreak on the animal world, not least in many films. But if animal film imagery contains elements that entail an ethical response, and if this response is enabled precisely by the manner in which a number of different, even contradictory, values are combined in film – science, entertainment, spectacular visuals, special effects and illusory images – then an interesting tension arises. Critics of animal films have long observed an opposition between scientific and entertainment values, an opposition that usually translates across a series of polarities with truth (usually understood as objective scientific truth), education and detached observation on the one side and commerce, entertainment and pleasure on the other. However, the tensions are more complex than this. If anything the animal is overdetermined partly because the above factors cannot help but coincide, and partly because, as Crowson's remark indicates, the animal can easily be appropriated by the discourse of sublimity so important to traditions of visual aesthetics generally.

As with most aspects of animal films, the technical achievement of obtaining the right kind of footage, and often the advertisement of that achievement, increases the overall sense of the grandeur or spectacular in the imagery: magnification in all senses of the word. Watching a Tiger beetle for fourteen days to get a ten-second shot of egg-laying, for instance, entails more than just the achievement of a fascinating and instructive shot. This episode combines all sorts of different registers from the strict discipline of patient observation to the mismatched scales of time and size. In other words, the grandeur of the film combines both a sense of rigidity and a shift in the normal modes by which we perceive things. In fact, the magnified filming of insects for nature films easily echoes genres such as horror and science fiction.[4] Claude Nuridsany and Marie Perennon, the directors of *Microcosmos* (1996), a film about 24 hours in the life of insects in a meadow, cited science fiction rather than documentary as the genre most inspirational to their film. Nuridsany wanted the insects to be viewed as like neither animals nor humans but as figures from another planet. This film was the product of considerable labour, including fifteen years of scientific work and three years of filming.[5] Special kinds of cameras were required, including a light-weight camera mounted inside a remote-controlled helicopter to follow the flight of a dragonfly.[6] The film itself is a collage of all sorts of different types of imagery, some of which play on comedy – the dung beetle whose piece of dung gets stuck on a twig causing it all sorts of problems – to bizarre close-ups and even a point-of-view shot, made up of coloured polygons, through the eyes of a flying insect. There is no documentary style voiceover so throughout one is being asked to look without necessarily understanding what one sees. Despite the fact that *Microcosmos* uses highly sophisticated technology, some of it developed specifically to deal with problems presented by the material, the overall mixed format reflects a tradition going back to some of the first full-length nature documentaries. Charles Urban, for instance, produced two important examples of mixed format film in the 1920s: *The Four Seasons* (1921) and *Evolution* (1926). *The Four Seasons*, made by Raymond Ditmars over a period of three years, showed animals and flora at different times of the year and, as one advertising pamphlet put it,

A poster advertising Charles Urban's mixed format film *The Four Seasons* (1921).

A poster for Charles Urban's film *Evolution* (1926).

'living a year in an hour but only growing an hour older'.[7] In fact, the compression of time also had advantages for holding public attention. As Urban noted, 'to a scientist . . . the picture of a bird's development from birth is an interesting study, but it would be too long and tiresome to hold public interest, and for that reason we have taken small "shots" and woven them together along different themes'.[8] In his film *Evolution* Urban went even further and used a mix of models, 'animated glimpses' of dinosaurs, material from the American Museum of Natural History, footage shot in the Bronx Zoo and other pieces of film to present the history of the universe. The opening begins by showing how man has harnessed the elements, with footage of things like trains and aeroplanes. It also depicts the near collision of two solar bodies, the formation of the earth and includes pictures of everything from ameoba to the higher mammals. The English version ends with man's highest achievement: the Houses of Parliament.[9] Urban did not court any controversy by invoking Darwin in the film but simply presented a montage of images around a temporal narrative which culminated in human triumph. Interestingly, one newspaper advertisement noted that the Tennessee high court was then deciding on whether to allow an anti-evolutionary statute in the light of the Dayton Trial. This film would, the paper announced, interest everyone whatever their personal thoughts on the controversial subject of evolution. However, the paper also added that the film had been re-edited for popular release eliminating all 'technical terminology and scenes which delved too deeply into the subject for the layman'.[10] But although Urban might not have wanted to court controversy in his production of what was meant primarily to be appealing entertainment, the scale of the spectacle was intended to inspire an appreciation of the living world, in the same way that Nuridsany and Perennon wanted their audience to see the insect world with different eyes via the marvel of their magnified footage.

Another version of ethical animal 'seeing' can be found in the combination of an interest in the aesthetics of the whole animal body with the idea that the pursuit of this interest is in some way morally and physically beneficial. As with the examples mentioned above, scientific knowledge is not necessarily essential to this kind of seeing and is deemed by some writers to be secondary to a kind of visual knowledge understood to be adequate in its own right. This has a long historical tradition. Books and periodicals that relate to still photography of animals in the 1890s and early 1900s often cover matters of technique and approaches deemed appropriate to the filming of wildlife, such as patience and care, without necessarily being interested in detailed scientific issues about the wildlife as such. After all, this was a practice that was concerned with seeing more without necessarily knowing more and points to an important distinction between the visual and the textual animal, in this case articulated in science. Using a camera, as one photographer noted in 1914, means 'that we learn much that would pass otherwise unnoticed, and make records that are, or should be, infinitely more useful than any sketch or written note could be'.[11] The practice of nature photography was also considered wholesome in terms of its celebration of the outdoors. In keeping with a more general long-standing discourse that linked fresh air to moral health, nature photography was described as an activity that took people into the countryside, giving relief to the mind and health to the body: 'If the charm of nature study were better known to the young people in our large towns, many would become students, and much of the waste and dissipation of town life would lose its attraction in the healthier pursuit of studying wildlife in the field.'[12] The implication was that one form of modern technology, the camera, could be used to escape from other effects of modernity. Furthermore, animal photography required a great deal of time and patience, in direct antithesis to an accelerating pace of life. The place of the photographer in the landscape was also important particularly as he or she should be as invisible and non-interventionist as possible.[13] It was recommended, for instance, that one should not cut away the foliage in bird-nest photography for more light, as it would leave the nest unprotected. And yet, although this type of photography was understood by some as a retreat from modernity, the growing number of animal illustrations in magazines and journals and the increasing popularity of pet photography, especially from the last quarter of the nineteenth century onwards, meant that it also fed an increasing mass market for animal imagery.[14] By 1900, according to Guggisberg, there were 256 camera clubs, including a number devoted to animal photo-

The invisible photographer: Cherry Kearton photographing from his brother Richard's shoulders and, below, from within a model cow.

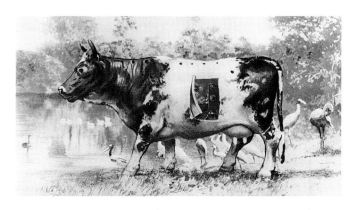

The invisible photographer: wildlife photographer Frank Newman at work, c.1914.

graphy and an estimated 4 million camera owners.[15] We can see here a contradiction between avoiding the stresses of modernity through the retreat into nature whilst at the same time contributing to the mass representation of animals.

Alongside the idea that the photography of nature was good for one's moral health there was another important ethic: that the use of the camera was superior to the gun both morally and in terms of the craft of getting close to wildlife. This was in many respects a commonplace frequently mentioned not only by photographers but also by zoologists and many others. Scholars from a number of perspectives have analysed the resemblances between the camera and the gun, including the question of shared similarities in design and the parallels between the trophy and the photograph.[16] But there is a further significance in this outlook which lies

'Sport on the Cinematograph', 1909.

in conceptions, shared by both hunter and photographer, of the relationship of the human to the animal world in terms of proximity and even identification. The photographer A. Radclyffe Dugmore remarked that the camera 'leads to greater "intimacy" with nature' which seems an appropriate way to describe the kinds of stalking needed to obtain photographs. It was not enough to get even nearer to the prey than was necessary for a gunshot; photographers also needed to

One of George Shiras's cameras triggered by tripwire, c.1900.

set the camera right and hope for a 'suitable attitude'.[17] In other words more care was needed than for hunting. Like hunters, cameramen such as R. B. Lodge and George Shiras also used trip wires linked to automatic camera shutters around the turn of the century just as Muybridge had done in his galloping horse series of 1878.[18] In fact, Shiras extended the possibilities of animal photography when he linked his trip wire system to flash, producing the memorable night-time photographs that won him a Gold Medal at the Paris World Exhibition in 1900.[19] Thus, both photography and hunting involved similar kinds of practical

Cherry Kearton, 1942.

Doug Allan filming polar
bears on Hopen Island,
Svalbard, Norway.

knowledge and skill, concerning locations, habits and the visual identification of creatures. The main difference was that, ideally, photography should leave no mark on the environment and the key relationship between human and animal was non-interventionist and purely visual. In practice the situation was different, as Cherry Kearton noted when he remarked on the visible reduction of African game since 1913, which he blamed partly on settlers and partly on 'a certain type of photographic expedition or safari'.[20]

Early efforts to capture animal movement photographically brought ethical issues into a relationship with photographic technology more tangentially. This was an ethical or humane enterprise in that these were investigations into the whole animal body carried out, as far as possible, under free conditions of movement. Of course, this was often difficult. For instance, Muybridge photographed animals extensively at the zoo in Philadelphia in 1884 and 1885, although he recognized the limitations of the setting:

> It would have been desirable, however, to have photographed many of the animals while they were enjoying more freedom of movement than that afforded by the Gardens of the Zoological Society, but the difficulties attending a satisfactory investigation under their natural conditions of life were, at the time, too great to be surmounted.[21]

The scientific potential of this work was therefore somewhat limited, although his photographic sequences of zoo animals were analysed by scientists to establish similarities and differences in the locomotion of different species.[22] Jules-Etienne Marey was also not averse to borrowing animals from the zoo and Marta Braun describes his laboratory, the Station Physiologique in the Bois de Boulogne, in 1892 as a combination of farm and aviary.[23]

The history of the first attempts to capture animals in motion is well known, so I will describe it only briefly here.[24] Eadweard Muybridge began his studies of the movement of horses, which would eventually lead to his photographic sequences of animals in motion, in 1872 at the behest of Leland Stanford, the president of Central Pacific Railroad, and one-time governor of California. The aim was to establish the nature of the horse's gallop. The initial intention was to decide whether there was a point at which all four hooves left the ground during the gallop and to apply this knowledge to understanding and optimizing the running of horses in races.[25] Initially Muybridge used a single camera, but developed increasingly sophisticated shutter mechanisms to capture the horse in motion. In his later work, from 1878 onwards, Muybridge improved his system by using banks of cameras, the shutters of which were triggered by the horses' hooves breaking threads laid across the track. Muybridge was to stick to this basic principle for photographing moving bodies and continued increasing the numbers of cameras. For *The Human Figure in Motion*, published in 1901, he used three batteries of cameras operated by a motor clock that allowed for 24 photographs to be taken in a quarter of a second. This meant also that he could take the same moving object from different angles.[26] The German Ottomar Anshütz initiated his studies of aerial locomotion in 1882 using a similar system to that of Muybridge, with up to 12 cameras side by side. Military interest in his work led to his undertaking photographic series on equine and aerial locomotion for the Prussian army from 1885.[27] This was not, however, the only photographic method employed. Jules-Etienne Marey, when first attempting to photograph birds in flight, used a camera that was based on the design of a rifle with a single circular rotating photographic plate.[28]

Because images that Muybridge, Anshütz and Marey produced are often seen in terms of the wider history of the technologization of the body and the relationship between movement and efficiency – so important to theorizing the interaction between bodies and the needs of industry – the centrality of animals to their projects has been substantially ignored.[29] Also, as we saw in the first chapter, the coincidence of Muybridge's animal studies with his studies of naked women elided the human and animal body under a similar visual structure: the voyeuristic, eroticized and objectifying gaze (in spite of the fact that many of the animal bodies, particularly those filmed against the geometrical grids that marked the backdrops, appear out of context, and, above all, devoid of any human connotation). Marey shifted during his scientific career from his initial interest in devices to register the internal processes of the animal, such as the

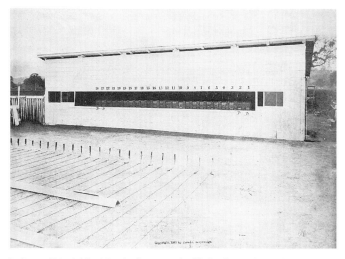

Eadweard Muybridge's bank of cameras for filming horses in motion, *c.* 1881.

Otto Anschuetz's electrical tachyscope (an early animated picture machine), as seen in *Scientific American*, 1889.

heartbeat, to the examination of external movements. This was, whatever the nature of Marey's private feelings towards animals, a move towards a less physically invasive and thus more humane scientific observation of the animal body. He was indeed a critic of vivisection, although primarily on the scientific grounds that it was ultimately dependent on visual examination which in itself was fatally flawed, and only second because it was damaging to the object of scientific investigation. However, the constant in his work was his focus on the mechanics of bodies and the creation of devices to inscribe such dynamics. Hence his interest in the action of the wings of birds, and even the movement of the fins of the skate in water, which he also filmed, for the understanding of aerodynamics. Expanding the extent to which the animal could be seen enhanced the envisaging of certain types of machine. It will be clear that this is a science of surfaces in which, crucially, consideration of the whole animal body is of primary importance. Thus, whilst the impulse behind the photography is mainly scientific, the particular figuration of the animal body is as an active, dynamic whole which is at its most instructive when free to move. This is a very different knowledge producing practice from physiology, which needs to damage or destroy the animal body to reach its conclusions.

Although there are parallels between Marey's and Muybridge's sequential photography of animals, the two men differed in their motivation. Marta Braun, in her study of Marey, claims that Marey and Muybridge represent two

Chronophotographic
picture of horse's
hooves taken by
Jules-Etienne Marey,
c. 1892.

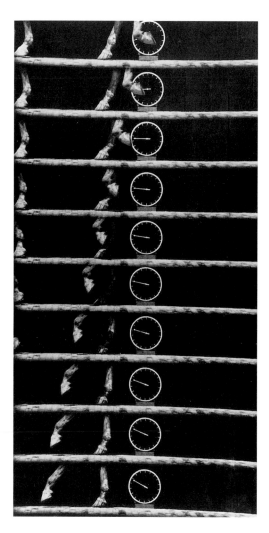

A horse and trap in motion, in one of Eadweard Muybridge's early photograph sequences, c. 1880s.

complementary strands of motion photography. She contrasts the disinterested, analytic and science-orientated approach of Marey to the narrative, aesthetic and dramatic sensibilities of Muybridge. However, if anything Marey's animal photographs, with their blurring of successive movements, are more aesthetically striking than those of Muybridge. Equally, Muybridge's more extensive documentation of species, which aimed towards a classification of zoological locomotion, could be said to be just as scientifically revealing about particular creatures as the work of Marey. They each drew different conclusions, due to their different backgrounds, concerning the benefits of this kind of photography. Muybridge saw his work as a supplement to vision, enabling, amongst other things, artists to portray movement accurately, whereas Marey was more concerned to reveal that

Film of a falling cat taken by Jules-Etienne Marey, 1894.

which could not be seen. For both men it was a question of seeing more. These sequential photographic series are a significant part of the history of the technological development of moving film and the animal imagery shares specific features common to both still and moving photography.

The early photographic experiments to depict movement, by getting animals to parade past the camera, anticipate the frameworks of early moving film. Despite the striking novelty of moving film itself, the sequences derive from seeing animals in ordinary contexts: in the street, at the racetrack or in the cage. These are the visual horizons of the very first animal moving film imagery between 1895 and 1900: those of arenas (horse-races, bullfights, circuses), the city streets (parades, ceremonies, transport) and zoos.[30] This

Messrs. Bostock & Wombwell's Royal Menagerie on the road.

Bostock and Wombwell's Royal Menagerie entering Bootle, Cumberland, c. 1900; a still from a film distributed by Charles Urban.

is another reason why it is important not to elide analysis of the filming of animals with the filming of humans. Marey's photography of birds using his photographic gun and Muybridge and Stanford's interest in the racing horse also show that aspects of the hunt (the tracking shot) and the pursuit are just as important in structuring this form of photography as they are in informing photographic practices in the wild. In other words, these projects are not simply informed by science but are linked to more practical engagements between human and animal. This too should remind us why it is important not to conflate the scientific project of knowing more about animals with the visual project of seeing more.[31] The fragmented viewpoints of photographic series and the elements of anti-institutional science in amateur still photography (the photographic record that is superior to the text) point towards, as well as create, many different kinds of knowledge of animals.

It is tempting to envisage a historical account by which one can move easily from the animal imagery of Muybridge and Marey to the first animal moving films. However, as Brian Winston points out, there are many dangers in this given the complexities of the cinematograph's technological history.[32] Nevertheless, there is no doubting the significance of the visual animal body to the technologies of modernity, particularly those such as film, which also shape modernity's sense of itself. Consider, for instance, François Dagognet's claim that Marey's work foreshadowed many of the foundations of the modern world: 'the signals and fluxes, the multiple tele-inscriptions . . . and, more obviously, travel in the air (airplanes) and underwater; the capacity to preserve traces; abstract art and the crucial domain of audiovisual communication.'[33] In her book *Screening the Body*, Lisa Cartwright claims that the imaging of the living active body at the end of the nineteenth century is linked to the disciplining of that body, particularly at the conjunction of cinema and science. In fact, she sees sequential photography and early cinema as having historical precedents in the non-visual means of recording and measuring bodily mechanisms as exemplified, for example, by the early devices of Marey.[34] Although I do not consider this to be a true lineage for animal photography, because of the equal importance of non-scientific contexts, the argument has an important implication: the dynamic representations of animals on film were both an indication of a more humane science and an expression of an increased control over all aspects of life. This does not mean that there was not also a darker side to animal filmmaking, as Cartwright's own examples of Braun's 1898 film of an exposed and beating dog's heart or Edison's well-known *Electrocuting an Elephant* of 1903 indicate.[35] However, this double-edged issue of an increase in control over animal bodies, in a variety of contexts from science to legislation, alongside expressions of a more humane approach towards them, is unavoidably played out in film. One version of this, which is indeed crucial to the sequential photographic project, concerns the question of free or mechanical movement and this, too, is of significance in early moving film.

Two scenes from Cecil Hepworth's film *Rescued by Rover* (1905).

One of the first animal hero films ever made was entitled *Rescued by Rover* (Hepworth, 1905) and it opens with the dog, a collie, watching over a baby. The film is composed of a series of brief sequences. The nanny goes out walking with the baby in a pram and refuses to give money to a woman vagrant. She is then distracted by the attentions of a soldier, with whom she shares a cigarette, and the tramp steals the baby. The nanny returns home distraught and tells the mother. Rover enters the picture and then sets off to search for the baby, running down the street, crossing a river and entering a house. The next scene sees the vagrant returning to her room and she starts undressing the baby, examines the clothes, then sits down with a bottle. At this point Rover enters the room, finds the baby and makes off with an item of clothing. We then follow the dog as it retraces its route and returns to the house. He tries to attract the attention of the father who finally notices the item of clothing (tied) on the dog's back. Again the film follows the sequence of Rover's route, this time with the father in pursuit. The father retrieves the baby leaving the woman to her bottle, and in the final shot the family is re-united with the trusty Rover in the centre of the shot, still with the baby's clothing attached, and the nanny nowhere to be seen.

Most of the themes found here are recognizable from many subsequent fictional animal films, in particular the idea of the all-knowing animal healing a loss within the family. In this instance moral themes such as the unreliability of women and the perils of drink are to the fore, and it is noteworthy that Rover returns to get the father, rather than the nanny or the mother, to follow him to the baby. I shall discuss these familial motifs at greater length in the final chapter. However, it is the significance of the chase *in relation to* particular codes of conduct that I wish to highlight here. The sequence of the pursuit has a repetitive structure whereby the dog is shown following the same route three times. Relevant here is Jonathan Auerbach's argument concerning the regressive elements and repetitions of chase sequences in his study of pursuit films around 1904–5.[36] The repetition of movements, and the idea that this pursuit is caused by a set of events (the weakness of women) beyond the control of the pursuers (i.e. the father and the dog), implies that the movements are more mechanistic than volitional, though this becomes relative when the father has to imitate the movements of the dog. However, there is an additional element here, particularly highlighted by silent film, which concerns the absence of spoken language. The father has to understand the gestures of Rover, just as the audience has to understand the gestures of the humans in the film, and follow the dog accordingly. This he fails initially to do until he sees the item of clothing on the dog's back. The shared understanding of human and animal is therefore expressed visually and reinforced by an identity of action, all of which take place outside the realm of language. In this film it is the dog that is the possessor of knowledge: Rover is the only figure on the screen who 'understands' as much as the camera. One can see in this example how the themes of the mechanical (the pursuit) and the non-mechanical (the possibility of a common understanding outside of language) come together without actually collapsing into each other. Furthermore, in common with the way film inevitably derives from other aspects of human–animal relations, the structure of the hunt, though not particularly evident, can be faintly discerned.

Garry Marvin's study of fox-hunting is helpful here. In the English fox-hunt, there are complex patterns of identification between pack and prey as the hunt follows the trail set by the fox. Most importantly it is the pack of dogs that follow the fox, and the horsemen that follow the pack. The flight of the fox determines the route the hunt takes and the hunt should not get ahead of the fox or attempt to ambush it. These patterns of identification need not be understood in psychological terms. It is irrelevant, for example, how the hunt members, or even hounds for that matter, might subjectively conceive of the fox. Rather the identification can be registered in the visual and physical configurations of the hunt as it moves as a unit *with* the fox.[37] In that sense hunting embodies, among other things, forms of mimicry. Another version of this is the nature photographer's ideal of invisibility as s/he stalks animal-like through the landscape. In other words, it is when hunting that humans behave most like animals.

Derek Bousé has noted a transition in animal films at the turn of the century from the many animal 'feeding' films in the period of 1898 to 1905, which were 'virtually eventless

Tiger and bull fight at San Sebastien, Spain, c. 1905; a still from a film distributed by Charles Urban.

and did not even provide a rudimentary basis for narrative development', to hunting films with 'their greater dramatic, and therefore narrative possibilities'. 'Feeding was quickly replaced by hunting, stasis by action, and ultimately, nurturing by killing.'[38] This is to some extent true but requires qualification. Dramatic structures can be found in the very earliest animal films. Indeed it makes more sense to see the transitions in animal films in visual terms, rather than in plot terms, particularly in the opening up of the visual horizons within which animals are contained. The photography of animal death, for instance, is extended to more open horizons from Africa to the Arctic, particularly towards the end of the first decade of the twentieth century. This can be seen in the work of Cherry Kearton in Africa and the Italian filmmaker

Luca Comerio, whose travelogues from all over the world contain many killing scenes. As I've mentioned, the earliest moving films cover a multitude of subjects such as animals in zoos, animals moving past a camera on a street, either as draught animals or in parades, or in sporting arenas such as the horse race, cock fighting, boxing cats and kangaroos ('Boxing Cats, an interesting and scientific bout between two trained Thomas Cats'), and bullfights.[39] These generated considerable interest. As F. A. Talbot noted in 1912, the 1896 Derby re-run on the screen at the Alhambra Theatre in London 24 hours after the race caused more excitement than the race itself.[40] These early animal films are more than mere depictions of movement, and are structured in quite specific ways. In the pre-1900 zoo films, for instance, one sees subjects like pelicans walking into water, a lion being attracted to a piece of meat that a keeper is waving in front of his bars, or an elephant being washed. Even at a rudimentary level there is still the sense of organized event. Whether in parade footage or the thrill of the bullfight, animal subjects reinforced the excitement and novelty of moving imagery itself with their own potential for spectacle. Many of the tropes that later surfaced in safari and hunting films, such as exoticism and even animal death, were already in place.

In an early film of a Spanish bullfight (1895) the sequence of events displayed on the film is structured with a beginning, middle and end.[41] The film begins with the parade. Initially we see three men on horseback, and then a horse-drawn carriage followed by the matadors, picadors, toreadors and others. At the very back of the parade one can just make out the horses and harnesses used for dragging dead carcasses from the arena. This is followed by the initial appearance of the bull, different aspects of the fight itself beginning with various shots of the matadors attempting the kill, a picador readying himself for his attack, and finally some footage of combat with the toreadors. At the very end, in keeping with a faint symmetry that runs throughout the film, the carcass of a horse is dragged around the edge of the arena by a team of horses. The shots of the matador are almost exclusively concerned with attempts at the kill, rather than the earlier manoeuvres that are integral to the art of the bullfight. This is no surprise, given that most animal films are concerned with compressing animal activities to highlight their most visually interesting forms. This contrast between the ritual of the parade and the thrill of the sudden charges and threats of the bull is reminiscent of other hunting films. Another version of this are the kinds of film in which, say, a scene of a staged gladiatorial combat between big cats in an enclosure is inserted into footage of a hunt. The framing of the kill or the fight as a particular episode within the hunt itself again reflects visual codes particular to the structure of hunting itself.

In Pathé's *Buffalo Hunting in Indo-China* (1908) the film begins with a version of the meet. A group of Europeans with their servants move off on horseback or in carriages in the foreground whilst in the background they are watched by men on elephants and villagers. Then there is a parade past the camera by the Europeans and some of the locals on the elephants, with the villagers following. In these shots the camera waits for everyone to pass by until the last figure has left the screen. Scenes in the film are carefully composed on this model with the white men and their assistants in the front and the elephants behind. In line with the ethos of pitting the skill and courage of the single hunter at the kill – the idea of individual combat – in this killing sequence only one man is shown firing at the water buffalo, which is killed and eventually pulled out of the water by the elephants. The final shot has the hunters standing around the carcass with the villagers standing behind them looking over the shoulders of the hunters. The patterns of imperialism and human order that are reflected in the visual organization of the different scenes remind us how important it is to see the practice of hunting and animal killing as always in some way troped.[42] It is these rules and codes that distinguish hunting from simply killing. It also means that film structurally reproduces the hunting ethic, which exonerates the killing of animals on film whilst reproducing the thrill of the hunt. This point raises a much bigger question about the interplay between the manner in which human–animal relations are coded, even when they might appear to be explicitly raw and direct, and the manner in which these relations are understood to reproduce processes found in nature, such as hunting, killing, eating or bodily display. There is a double ethic at work here. On the one hand, culture civilizes the practice of hunting by means of various codes of conduct and ritual

Lassoing a rhino-
ceros, filmed by
Cherry Kearton
in 1911.

while, on the other hand, the practice appears justified in
nature given that, as the animal conflict footage shows,
combat and killing are common throughout the animal
kingdom.

In addition to the kind of ethic at work in hunting
films, natural history films more generally were seen as
important in reinforcing moral values and improving the
social tone of the cinema in the early twentieth century.[43]

'Animal Vegetarians' from the Animal Kingdom series; a disk of images to be screened on the Urban-Joy Spirograph home-projector, designed by Charles Urban in 1913 but not marketed until the 1920s.

Amongst the early filmmakers in Britain, Charles Urban most exemplifies this.[44] An American who arrived in England in 1896 and moved into film production with the founding of the Warwick Trading Company a year later, Urban was an important figure in the making of early nature and animal films. He was himself a keen keeper of birds, having a large aviary at his home in England that he also used for filming. It was no coincidence that he presented a more socially respectable face to filmmaking. Just as animals were so crucial to technological developments in film, they were also very important to the debate about the public morals of the cinema. As Charles Urban's surviving correspondence and his invitations to dignitaries demonstrate, his films gained a great deal of social respectability. This was partly

through his production of a mixture of films, covering imperial military topics and royal occasions, as well as animal and
scientific subjects. An exhibition of animal pictures at the
Zoological Society of London in 1910 noted that these films
'had been exhibited hitherto in this country only before their
Majesties the King and Queen at Knowsley, the Society of
Arts, and the Palace Theatre, London. The pictures had been
taken, with one or two exceptions, at the Society's Gardens in
Regent's Park and at the National Zoological Park, Washington.'[45] Many of these films were simple sequences of shots of
animals. However, in producing the time-lapse, microscopic
and trick photography of filmmakers such as Percy Smith
and F. Martin Duncan, Urban also exploited the mutually
reinforcing novelty of both technology and subject matter.
These films make use of a distinctive combination of home-
liness and technological innovation in, for instance, microscopic films of topics like pond life, cheese mites and the
risks to human health posed by the fly, and yet they also
pushed the current technical limits and imaginative possibilities of film. As the *Telegraph* noted in 1915, 'Up-to-dateness
is further exemplified by a number of pictures entitled "The
menace of the fly" . . . by the far the most extraordinary part
of this film is a section of photographs taken through the
lenses of a fly's eye, thus giving an idea of how the fly sees his
mortal enemy – man.'[46] In the public presentation of
Urban's first productions of colour cinematography in 1909,
in which filming was done through rotating tinted lenses, it
was films of zoo animals that most impressed the critics.[47]

Still from one of the trick insect films made by Percy Smith, c. 1911; the film was screened upside down to show the fly juggling a cork.

These films reflect a very different tradition from the hunting and safari films and represent a much more local, domestic, vision of nature. This kind of filming was more controllable, but in another sense produced greater challenges in keeping its subject matter interesting. In the end many of these films dated rather quickly, as indicated by F. A. Talbot's remark in 1923, that a decline in the popularity of nature films was partly the result of the audience becoming jaded with what was seen as trick photography.[48] That there was something of a decline in the demand for educational films after World War One is also remarked on by Cherry Kearton. Remembering Charles Urban's films in 1935 he wrote:

> It is odd to remember that in those days to call a film 'educa-
> tional' was a real advertisement for it, whereas now any
> educational quality is considered the greatest drawback
> which must be either omitted altogether or disguised under
> the cloak of 'entertainment' so that it is unrecognizable.[49]

The use of photographic trickery was part of the
process of highlighting novelty and finding interesting
angles on subject matter that were closer to home, such as
insects or plants. As Talbot noted, filmmakers had
laboured 'under the delusion that it was only wild and
unfamiliar life, amid natural environments, which would
command popular approval'.[50] The development of this
type of filmmaking was made up of a number of strands,
which partly derived from the illusory-style cinema of
filmmakers like Meliès, as exemplified in trick films of
insects juggling objects, and partly from a fascination with
contraptions in conjunction with amateur nature study.[51]
Percy Smith, an officer with the Board of Education until
he began his work with Charles Urban in 1908, exploited
the possibilities of microscopic and time-lapse photography to make the invisible visible and the commonplace
unusual. His time-lapse film, *Birth of a Flower* (1911), was
a great success and he went on to make similar films, many
of which were made in his home in Surbiton, including
one of the growth of mould (the spread of which was
eventually to threaten the fabric of his own house).
Smith's contraptions were made up of all sorts of bits and

A slow action outdoor camera used by Percy Smith, *c.* 1910.

Percy Smith operating an elaborate indoor camera, *c.* 1939.

Setting a *Secrets of Nature* film to music, 1930.

A still from Ernest Schoedsack and Merian Cooper's *Chang: A Drama of the Wilderness* (1927).

pieces, including cogs and chains, bicycle pedals, gramophone needles and parts of different cameras. To avoid the possibility of losing footage for long time-lapse shoots he would also attach alarms to the cameras in case they broke down. One result was that plant life was brought into the same time and action frame as animals. Smith's output was diverse, as his list of some of his own films in his 1911 notebook reveals: for instance, *Tiny Honey Gatherers*, *Snakes and their Habits*, *Peculiar Pets*, and *Fun in a Bear Pit*. This in turn set the tone for most of his later work and continued when he joined the *Secrets of Nature* project in 1924.[52] These were short films on a variety of natural history topics of eight to ten minutes in length, though they could take anything from three months to four years to make.[53] Smith's career – he died in 1945 – was marked by the constantly fluctuating status of 'educational' films, although they offered a completely different aesthetic from the more spectacular animal footage to be found in high profile films like Cooper and Schoedsack's *Grass* (1925) and *Chang* (1927).[54] His was an aesthetic that played on the surprise of the ordinary and reflected the local accessibility of the natural world. It was also an aesthetic that rejected the violence of much nature imagery and celebrated the underdog: 'if I think anything is a pest I make a film about it; then it becomes beautiful'.[55] The spirit of such films is summarized by one writer: 'although correct in detail, they are not made by experts or scientists, but by ordinary people for ordinary people and are therefore not dull, opinionated, high-brow or condescending'.[56]

Advertising the moral virtues of nature film was not without commercial interest, particularly as these films were aimed at widening cinema audiences and encouraging the idea that cinema entertainment could be respectable. In an advertising listing for one of Urban's animal films, the films are described as 'an offset to the irksome "blood and thunder" films with which the cinema trade is inundated'. Urban also pointed out that his kinds of film could be of benefit to animals themselves. In a pamphlet he wrote entitled *The Cinematograph in Science, Education, and Matters of State*, dated April 1907, he suggested that film records of operations on animals would decrease the need for vivisection.[57] In 1917, the National Council for Public Morals published a study of the cinema in which they expressed their concern about the impact of cinema on society and the importance of natural history films in improving the overall quality of film programmes. However, they also recognized that these films could not compete against, for instance, Charlie Chaplin films or the *Exploits of Elaine* unless they had 'interests other than the purely educational'.[58] In other words, the popular aspects of natural history films were a necessity understood by all in the film business. As Talbot wryly remarked, even 'certain naturalist cinematographers declared the completely natural conditions to be a detracting feature from the popular point of view'.[59] The conflict, between desire and pleasure, on the one hand, and the public good and educational values, on the other, has been debated from the very earliest days of filmmaking. It is, incidentally, a debate that was exactly paralleled in debates over written animal stories in the early twentieth century, especially amongst American nature writers.[60] However, there is a particular significance to the debate over nature films, since it reveals that animal imagery was felt to be socially important enough to be worth regulating in the same way that other forms of film imagery were regulated in relation to sexuality and blasphemy, for example.

The regulation of animal imagery is seen most overtly in formal systems of censorship. As we shall see during the rest of this chapter, this has consequences both for what is seen on screen, as well as in other aspects of film production,

W. S. Van Dyke's film *Trader Horn* caused outrage in some quarters for its depiction of hunting and animal death.

Two hunting scenes from *Trader Horn*.

such as training animals and even the history of special effects. In Britain, film censorship on the grounds of cruelty to animals has a long history dating back to 1913 and the inception of what was initially called the British Board of Film Censors (BBFC), now the British Board of Film Classification. In the first annual report of 1914 'cruelty to animals' was the first of 22 grounds for cuts or rejection.[61] As the BBFC expanded its criteria for excision in subsequent years, it also increased the number of clauses concerning animals and made them more specific. In 1919, these included cock-fighting, the branding of animals and, bizarrely, images of animals gnawing men and children.[62] In James Robertson's studies of British censorship, he lists a number of animal films that were subject to various degrees of censorship, including *A Spanish Bullfight* (1900); *Island of Lost Souls* (1932); *Trader Horn* (1930), an adventure film made in Africa which included footage of animals being killed and animal fights; and *The Hounds of Zaroff* (1932), in which dogs are used to hunt down people on an island. It is worth just mentioning in particular the *Island of Lost Souls*, which was based on *The Island of Dr Moreau* by H. G. Wells, because this film was rejected on grounds that touch on animal issues, albeit tangentially.

Although censors objected specifically to a scene in which a beast–human feeds animals in cages, the film did not depict any actual cruelty to animals as such.[63] However, the theme of the film was vivisection and it can be taken as an interesting illustration of British sensitivity to this issue.

The picture was submitted to the BBFC three times: in 1933, 1934 and 1951. Each time it was vigorously rejected, and in 1951 the viewer's report referred to it as a 'monstrosity'. It is of course possible that the subject of human experimentation raised in the film may have had particular resonances for the censors after World War Two. Paramount applied to the BBFC again in 1957, when the company sought permission finally to release it in Britain. In the margins of the letter of application is a recommendation that the reply should contain the following: '1. The idea is repulsive; 2. The results are pretty nasty; 3. The climax of the film is impossible.'[64] Eventually the BBFC granted the film a certificate in 1958 but not without protest:

> After the most careful consideration it was agreed that the basic idea of this film was no less repulsive than when it was viewed before; that the results in the development of human beings out of animals and the climax on the operating table rendered the film totally unsuitable for public exhibition in this country.[65]

The climax mentioned is when the beast people rise up against Dr Moreau, played by Charles Laughton, and take him into his laboratory to operate on him. Paramount's argument in reply was that the theme of the mad scientist creating monsters was a standard one and that many contemporary horror films were far worse.

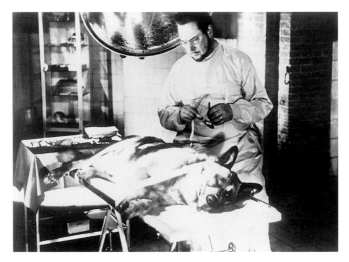

The scientist as vivisector in Georges Franju's film *Les Yeux sans Visage* (1959).

In fact the creation of world destroying forces, however fantastic the form in which they are presented, can be a far more frightening thing, in this age of advanced and fearful scientific experiment, than this story of experiments confined to a small island; a tale which is based on a book anyone can read.[66]

As Robertson points out, the film has rarely been shown in public in the United Kingdom, though it was recently released on DVD.[67] Rather like the film's own themes of hybridity and bestiality, there does appear to be something anomolous about this example, given that the film suggests the idea of vivisection rather than graphically showing it. However, the censorship is in keeping with a theme that runs throughout the history of animal violence on screen, in this case magnified by the monstrous figure of the beast–human, which is that the representation of such violence breaks the boundary between image and reality. Furthermore, it is the figure of the animal that seems to be the point at which they collapse. In other words, no matter how bizarre the manifestation of the idea of experimentation is, its appearance has the character of a visual taboo in twentieth-century British culture.

There are a number of dimensions to this issue of violence and cruelty on screen that are exacerbated by the moral onus placed on animal film imagery. The main problem lies in the problematic distinction between representation and 'reality', which is intensified by the technical artistry of film. The idea that animals represent an insertion of the real or the natural into film is crucial to the question of violence: 'Animals . . . have proved themselves among the best photographic subjects . . . Their naturalness and lack of camera or salary consciousness make their coming into a mechanistic melodrama or sentimental soufflé a refreshing restoration of the normal and the genuine.'[68] The commonplace that people are more sensitized to, or disturbed by, film violence involving animals than they are to that involving humans is difficult to assess or quantify, particularly in the absence of detailed studies of the impact of animal imagery on audiences. However, when such sentiments are expressed by people protesting against instances of screen violence, it does suggest that the suspension of belief that is normally in play with regard to humans on screen does not work in the same way for animals. The notion of the animal image as natural and the human image as one of artifice reiterates the traditional belief that animals are closer to the real than humans. Animal film imagery can highlight the making visible of violence. For a society that does not so much conceal violence as attempt to restrict it to its proper place, this unavoidable visual attention to its mechanics is inevitably problematic. This is reflected in the fact that from an early period legislation for the treatment of animals in films attempted to cover both the production process and the final imagery. In the bill for the Cinematograph Films (Animals) Act, which was worked on in early 1937, prohibition was suggested for 'any film depicting or purporting to depict combats with or between animals, or the suffering, terror or rage of animals.'[69] In other words, it was irrelevant whether the imagery was real or faked. By the time the Act was passed in July of that year, the position had been modified to include only the prohibition of suffering at the stage of production.

> No person shall exhibit to the public, or supply to any person for public exhibition . . . any cinematograph film (whether produced in Great Britain or elsewhere) if in connection with the production of the film any scene represented in the film was organized or directed

in such a way as to involve the cruel infliction of pain or terror on any animal or the cruel goading of any animal to fury.[70]

Another related argument, made by animal welfare campaigners, that also collapsed the boundary between representation and reality around the issue of violence, was that the impact of films involving animal violence would 'either arouse bloodlust or . . . cause indifference, especially in children, to the suffering of defenceless animals.'[71] This mention of children suggested that there were sections of the cinema audience more vulnerable to images of animal cruelty than others. This claim is, however, not simply based on the fear that children imitate what they see on screen. It also reflects a more fundamental belief that vision is the most impressionable and effective sense. In other words, the most natural route for knowledge to be taken in by the child is also the one most vulnerable to the corrupting influences of violence: 'childhood is pre-eminently the time of vision'.[72]

Animal combat in Frank Buck's *Bring 'Em Back Alive* (1932).

The dangerous power of images of violence inflicted on animals derives from what is perceived to be a potent mix of the natural and the visual, whether this violence is merely implied or properly realized on screen.

In 1939 E. K. Robinson, the secretary of the Our Dumb Friends League, wrote an article in *Sight and Sound* criticising the ineffectuality of the 1937 Act, as well as describing continuing brutalities in training methods.[73] He recommended the formation of a committee to regulate this aspect of the film industry and supervise trainers. This echoed a prescient remark made at the 1931 Performing and Captive Animals Defence League (PCADL) conference by an antivivisection campaigner, a Miss Schartan, who suggested that film producers should allow accredited representatives of animal protection societies to be present during the making of films involving animals.[74] This would eventually happen first in the United States from 1940 under the auspices of the American Humane Association. Robinson also repeated the idea that children were particularly vulnerable to certain kinds of animal film imagery and the possibility that they might consequently practise tricks on their pets. In sum, these sentiments during the 1930s represented a significant desire to police all aspects of the animal in visual culture.

Unease also extended to the depiction of animals fighting each other, whether it was contrived or took place in a natural context. Paradoxically, it was images of animal violence and not human violence that were understood to constitute a 'demoralizing and degrading experience'.[75] Was

Sergei Eisenstein filming
October (1927).

the implication that in extreme cases of uncivilized behaviour humans might become more animal-like? The legislative discussions of the animal image implicitly accept that it has the power to affect audiences in this manner. The violent animal image, therefore, has a significance that extends beyond simply representing the uncivilized (both in the sense of the 'natural' and the 'barbarous'), and, like a form of propaganda, is assumed to have the power to cause the repetition of such action. Again we see that the power of the animal film image stems from the fact that, because it is more prone to collapse the boundary of representation and reality than other forms of imagery, it threatens to reveal not just the isolated fact of coercion or cruelty but the whole system by which such coercion and cruelty are reproduced.

The creation of regulations for animal film imagery brings into play a whole series of codes, which make cruelty dependent on the framework in which it is presented. Certainly different genres of animal films (family stories, adventure and safari, natural history documentaries, medical films, animal rights topics, experimental and avant-garde films) have different criteria by which to judge what might be considered acceptable or unacceptable imagery. Hence the complex questions that arise in many of the debates on this topic. How is one to judge say, those natural history films that depict animal death by fighting, or even hunting in a natural environment? Would it be possible to evaluate from what is seen on film the manner in which such footage had been produced? And, an issue that seems to me of importance to the twenty-first century: Why is the depiction of cruel treatment to animals produced by welfare groups in their campaign films not also subject to considerations of sadistic voyeurism or indifference?

In 1931 the Performing and Captive Animals Defence League was launched to attack the whole principle of exhibiting animals. Their policy was to regard 'ALL professionally trained animal turns to be tainted with cruelty' and singled out the film *Trader Horn* for particular criticism.[76] They also campaigned for the BBFC not to grant any certifi-

Leaflet No. 1.
(THIRD EDITION.)

May, 1932.

CRUEL FILMS.

From a film passed by the British Film Censor, 1931.

THE ALLEGATIONS.—I.

(N.B.—It is not proposed to mention here the name of the film which was the immediate occasion of the following allegations, nor the name of the producing firm. The full facts originally appeared in Mr. Rob Wagner's "Script," a Hollywood film magazine of good standing and repute. Suffice it to say that both names were also published in an exposure in a British Sunday newspaper, "Reynolds's News," in December, 1931, without legal action being taken by the firm in question.

The cruelty inflicted is finished and done with; other firms have employed similar methods; and we are concerned with preventing its recurrence rather than with exposing the past actions of those whom we hope will set a much-needed example in the industry of film production.)

Cruel Films, a 1930s pamphlet by the Performing and Captive Animals Defence league attacking the principle of performing animals.

cate to a film depicting animals unless there was a written declaration by the filmmakers that 'no cruelty, brutality or restraint amounting to cruelty' was inflicted during the production.[77] At the 1931 conference mentioned above, this complex of thinking was reflected in a number of interventions. For instance, one speaker stated that he had shown a film of slaughter practices, but he had been glad to do so in order 'to show people what they were eating and that they were responsible for it.'[78] However, he had no objection to a film of seal killing because such animals were killed in the ordinary course of trade. Captain Fairholme, a high ranking member of the RSPCA and one-time secretary, further interjected that seal films did not apply anyway because they were 'trade films' and not 'cruel films'.[79] Another version of this effort to establish the rules for acceptable and unacceptable imagery along genre lines can be found in the desire to exempt medical or scientific film from the Cinematograph Films (Animals) Bill of 1937.[80] A further complication lay in the fact that there were different rules for different kinds of

This image of a dead horse with a trip rope around the base of its legs was used by the American Humane Association as part of their campaign.

A stunt rider causes a horse to fall on its side.

A horse can clearly be seen being tripped with a rope in Saimir Kumbaro's film *Vdekja E Kalit* (1992).

animals. The BBFC had been concerned, since 1912, about cruelty to *wild* animals, although wild animals were not covered by the 1911 Protection of Animals Act.[81] Hence their concern about whether 'kills' themselves should be shown and they concluded that as a general principle they should be avoided unless they appeared as one incident in a natural history film, 'and then only sufficient should be shown to indicate that such an incident has taken place'.[82] At a later conference, organized this time by the BBFC in May 1934, the chairman Edward Shortt remarked that 'we have always made the appearance of cruelty count as cruelty; we have equally made any restraint which appears in the treatment of animals count as cruelty.[83] After all, as Shortt noted, the BBFC could only base its judgements by what appeared on screen, though it was recognized that the problem of violence related to all levels of film from the question of its effects on audiences to its use in forcing animals to do things for the camera. Horror stories have always abounded about the various methods used to achieve certain effects: lions stirred into violent action by charging a wire meshed floor with electricity; binding the jaws of alligators with wire; or more recent claims concerning the training of horses with shock collars and pellet guns.[84] Nevertheless, although there are many exceptions, the overall history of filmmaking in the twentieth century does suggest that considerable progress has been made in improving the humane treatment of animals in film production. This is true especially, though not exclusively, of Britain and America. A number of different elements have contributed to this, including censorship and national legislation, as well as public responses to cruelty on film, and the activities of pressure groups.

Although the history of training animals for films is somewhat sketchy, scattered as it is through articles and largely anecdotal accounts, it does conform to the overall trajectory outlined above.[85] The line between coercion and training has been historically a subject of concern. One MP in the government debates over the bill for the 1937 Cine-matograph Films (Animals) Act echoed a common sentiment when he said, 'it is no facile sentimentality which considers the misuse of animals in films more distasteful than the misuse of men. The actor who is asked to endanger his life has the option of refusing and making the studio hire a stand-

Animators at Disney studying live penguins as an aid to animation.

The Selig company with its menagerie.

in or a double. But the animal has no choice.'[86] Concern for animal welfare in film production became increasingly regulated during the twentieth century, both via the application of legislation and the appearance of an increasing number of professional guidelines and organizational watchdogs. Although the circus and the zoo were the source of many trained or, hopefully, tractable animals for the first animal films, an industry devoted to providing trained animals for film was quick to develop. Talbot describes this as a 'new and curious profession', crediting the innovation to a young French animal trainer, Pierre Bourgeois. It involved things like training the animal to repeat simple movements such as crashing through a window into a room.[87] Some filmmakers and companies, such as Colonel Selig and Mack Sennett, had their own private menageries, exploited to the full in films

Animals at the PATSY awards, 1960.

like Vitagraph's *Wild Animals at Large*, in which a train wreck led to the escape of all the animals of a travelling circus.[88] In fact, Albert E. Smith, head of New York Vitagraph, hired two travelling menageries with more than 100 animals ranging from the lion to the monkey.[89] In 1915 Universal City established a zoo for jungle dramas, though it was closed in 1929 with the advent of sound, because it generated too much background noise for the recording engineers on other sets.[90]

The interaction between commercial and humane interests has also been an important factor in drawing attention to animals and their welfare. There was considerable profit to be made from trained animals, especially horses and dogs: in the 1920s dogs such as Strongheart, Rin Tin Tin, from the '40s onwards Lassie, and, more recently, modern canine stars like Benji.[91] The potential profit of these kinds of films, particularly when they cultivated the animal's stardom and encouraged public interest in the lives and health of their animal actors, was enormous. Eventually, from 1951, animals were awarded their own version of the Oscars, the PATSYs (Picture Animal Top Star of the Year), with the first award going to Francis, the Talking Mule.[92] Rin Tin Tin helped the financially struggling Warners in the 1920s; Bambi, admittedly not a live animal but still an iconic figure, was the hero of the top-grossing film of the '40s; the Disney nature films of the late '40s and '50s gave the company a new lease of commercial life; *Beethoven* (1992), a comic film about an oversized Saint Bernard, made $50 million.[93] Benji the dog made $1 million dollars income in the year 1986–7, whilst his film *Benji the Hunted* (1987) grossed $17 million in the first 24 days. The animal as a potential financial record breaker is also reflected in the success of films like *Jaws* (1975) and *Jurassic Park* (1993). Lions and other big cats were also commonly used. In 1932, for instance, *Picturegoer Weekly* carried the story of Charles Gay, an Englishman who ran the Hollywood Lion Farm. Initially he had bought many of Bostock's trained animals on the latter's death and taken them to Los Angeles. However, in response to a demand from producers for more realism and action rather than tricks, presumably in the aftermath of films like *Trader Horn*

A lion being filmed from within a cage, c. 1920s.

(1930), Gay got rid of these animals to focus on training lions specifically for more natural roles.[94]

From an overall point of view, it could be said that the pattern of the treatment of animals in film production has switched from one in which the requirements of the film-makers dictated the treatment of the animal to one in which the needs of the animal now dictate the programme of the filmmaker. This transition has not been a particularly smooth one. Working with wild animals, particularly in early films, could be as dangerous for the human as for the animal. During the shooting of the film *East of Java* (1935) a film made during a period of high popularity for 'fang and claw' movies, the star of the film was attacked and hospitalized. The footage from the attack was used in a promotional

Filming *Ben Hur*
(William Wyler,
1926).

Universal Newsreel and, although the Hays Office insisted the footage be cut from the actual film, some of the excised footage was still used for the preview trailer.[95] Rob Block, the owner of the training company Critters of the Cinema, remarked in an interview that animal training for show business originally attracted a very tough type of person: 'it was a heavy handed business in which people would kill an animal just to get a shot. Animals were just stock or props.'[96] In the 1925 version of *Ben Hur* some 150 horses were killed during the filming of the chariot race.[97] However, it was the reaction to the horse ridden off a 70-foot cliff in *Jesse James* (1939) that led to a contract between the American Humane Association (AHA) and the Hays Office giving the AHA the right to review scripts and have a representative on set to supervise the filming of animals.[98]

The power of the AHA has fluctuated. With the closure of the Hays Office in 1966, ironically a liberal move within the overall history of film censorship, the AHA's influence suffered accordingly and the organization noted a rise in dangerous techniques including, amongst other things, a reappearance of tripping wires for horses. In 1977 a clause was introduced into all film contracts allowing the AHA control, from the inception of a screenplay, over the use of animals. This signified a marked improvement in the organization's status.[99] However, there have been many films made since then that feature scenes deemed unacceptable; for instance, the slaughter of the water buffalo in *Apocalypse Now* (1979) and the cattle stampeding off a cliff in Ireland in

Lee Duncan gives hand signals to Rin Tin Tin, *c.* 1920s.

The Field (1990). The scale of the film industry makes close control over all film production extremely difficult, particularly as the AHA observes some 850 productions a year with a full-time field staff of only nine.[100]

In Britain, there has likewise been an increase in forms of regulation. Whereas once it was quite feasible to expect trainers to turn up to the studio without any prior warning of what was needed, now the animal agencies require exact instructions from directors and producers as well as themselves providing information on what is and is not possible.[101] Animals are often trained for specific purposes, which requires time and careful preparation. Although the logistics are not quite comparable, there is a marked contrast between the ethos under which Barbara Woodhouse would have turned up at a studio in the 1960s with her dog without having seen any script beforehand, and something like the preparation for the zoo comedy *Fierce Creatures* (1997), for which it took a year to organise the animals and complete all the relevant risk assessment paperwork.[102] Since the early 1960s there has also been a marked increase in the number of companies specializing in animal work. Many of these now work under the auspices of the Animal Consultants and Trainers Association, a body set up in 1989 to regulate fees in the profession and legitimize professional trainers.[103] Animal training is now an extensive industry that caters for every type of filmmaking, from feature films to advertising and pop videos. It uses all kinds of creatures, from anacondas to peacocks, seagulls to camels, or zebras to primates. The scale can vary from the high demands of, say, the Indiana Jones films (20,000 snakes, 8,000 rats, 3,000 cockroaches) to a small dog for a children's television programme.[104]

It is certainly valid to argue that the increasing attention to the care of animals in film production is not just a response to cultural shifts in attitudes to animal welfare. It is influenced by significant commercial considerations, given that charges of animal mistreatment are potentially damaging. Furthermore, the natural limitations of working with animals, such as animal fear or fatigue for instance, mean that a shoot efficiently planned around the animal saves time and money. Finally, this trend towards greater consideration for the animal comes hand in hand with increasingly self-conscious and self-reflexive forms of image production. As animal films become visually more sophisticated and versatile, particularly through the powerful combinations of live action, special effects and computer generated imagery (CGI), the process of creating this imagery becomes itself an object of attention and self-advertisement. To some extent this has always been the case, in the illustrated literature, both popular and academic, that comments on and advertises the film industry.[105] But the 'how it was done' footage that now accompanies the final product means that the animal image increasingly reflects the dimensions of its own artistry. Whether it is trivializing or intriguing to show the computer work that creates dinosaurs, or to reveal that it takes four months to train a dalmation to load a video tape into a VCR, is an open issue. There are all sorts of ramifications to the 'making of' footage that accompanied recent nature documentaries such as the BBC's *Walking with Beasts* and *The Blue Planet* (2001), the Attenborough documentary series on the oceans, and, more commonly, nature film DVDs, which frequently have additional commentaries by members of the production team and explanations of the techniques used in the film. Such materials highlight the constructed nature of the filming process and could be read as contributing to a process of displaying integrity in revealing how images are produced. Alternately, this is less a demystification of animal films than an aestheticization of their mechanics.

Jane Desmond has argued that approaches such as

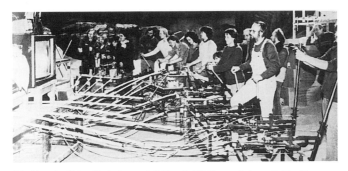

Working the flying 'luck dragon', Falkor, in Wolfgang Petersen's *The Never Ending Story* (1984).

Animatronics head used in Caroline Thompson's film *Buddy* (1997).

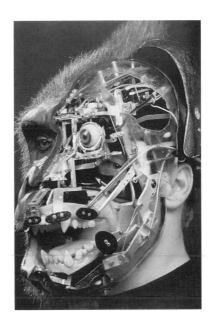

animatronics, in which the science of robotics is used to recreate the movements of bodies, are derived from a desire to recreate living animal bodies as taxidermy once did in the past. This is to some extent true.[106] But animatronics is only ever one component in the system that produces animal film imagery. Both now and in the past animal images have usually been put together using a collage of effects. Delmont's account of the film in which a live lion is replaced by a man dressed in a lion skin for the fight scenes is merely a crude version of the mixing of bodies and machinery that has so often characterized this kind of filmmaking.[107] This is paralleled by the way in which stock footage or material from other animal films is so often reused. Advances in technology have not necessarily changed this collage approach, even though with CGI they may do so eventually. *Jurassic Park* and its sequels, with their amalgamation of stop motion, animatronics and CGI, are some of the most striking recent examples, though they are part of a long tradition of dinosaur movies, from *The Lost World* (1925) onwards, that have pushed the boundaries of all sorts of tricks and techniques in filmmaking. Such films reveal the modern at the heart of the archaic. The animal is a central figure in other advances in film technique too. It can be found in the combination of camera movement and animation in *Who Framed Roger Rabbit?* (1988), another exercise in collage.[108] Popular dog films like *Fluke* (1995) used twelve different canines and an animatronic double, while *Man's Best Friend* (1993) used a combination of puppets (cable and remote controlled), plus a team of Tibetan mastiffs, whereby each dog was trained for one particular purpose, growling, jumping and so forth.[109] Body parts are also themselves interchangeable. In *The Ghost and the Darkness* (1996), a film vaguely based on John Patterson's book *The Man-Eaters of Tsavo* (1907), different model heads were placed on the lion bodies depending on the expression required; whilst in post-production the animals were then digitally recoloured, enhanced, and in some cases replaced completely by animation.[110] Humans inhabiting animal bodies are also subject to this increasingly sophisticated technical approach. In preparation for the film *Congo* (1995), the humans in gorilla outfits underwent a six-month training course to learn how to walk like mountain gorillas.[111] From an animal welfare point of view, there are many advantages to substituting models for live animals for difficult scenes. In *102 Dalmations* (2000), a film that also used live dogs, models and CGI, the neonate dogs suckling from their mother in one of the scenes were animatronic, and baby food was put on the models to encourage the mother to lick them. This particular strategem allowed new-born puppies to appear in the film (real ones would have been impossible for health reasons) whilst advertising the lengths to which a film company goes to affirm its welfare credentials.

In their book on the training of Lassie, Rudd Weatherwax and John Rothwell remarked that some of the most severe complaints about the treatment of dogs in *Lassie Come Home* (1943) came from Britain.[112] According to them, such complaints resulted from the public's failure to appreciate

A monster from Harry Hoyt's film *The Lost World* (1925).

the fact that scenes were contrived and the animals well-trained. The complaints were, in other words, a failure by the audience to accept the fictionality of the image. There are countless examples of this, which seems odd in the light of the publicity given to animal training and special effects. Richard Hill who provided the penguins for *Batman* made a similar point when people complained about the penguins, who had rockets firing from their backs or wore exploding headsets. All of this was in fact done using puppets.[113] In 1987 David Wilkins, the chief veterinary officer of the RSPCA, noted that although the treatment of animals on set had improved, the number of complaints had increased. He cited as an example objections to an advertisement for a cat food in which a budgie was balanced on a cat's head, although in fact both creatures were trained.[114] These responses by the public may be based on misunderstandings about the mode of production or based on a refusal to accept the playful or fictional imagery on the grounds that it is somehow inappropriate.[115] Either way, it still demonstrates that animal imagery is not seen in quite the same way as other forms of representation. That this reflects cultural attitudes to animals was a point recently made dramatically by the South Korean director Kim Ki-Deok in response to questions raised about episodes in his film *The Isle* (2000), in which the flanks were sliced off a live fish and a live frog was pulled apart. According to him, protests against these scenes merely revealed cultural differences between East and West.[116] This example locks into all the central themes of this chapter, showing how the animal image so often poses questions of ethics as an integral part of considering the technical conditions by which it is produced.

The conflict over acceptable and unacceptable animal imagery turns on the point at which, as I noted earlier, fiction and reality collapse into each other. Because the animal image is seen differently from the human image, the two cannot be compared in any simple sense. What is at one level a conflict over double standards is also a conflict over the symbolic status of the animal in relation to the meanings of film and its unstable, or conflicting, status as a visual image. In 2001 in Britain a scene was cut from Julian Schnabel's *Before Night Falls*. The scene involved a bird being caught and dragged through a hole in a prison roof, and was censored by the BBFC because, according to them, the bird appeared distressed. Schnabel commented: 'They [i.e. the prisoners] do to the bird what has been done to them. They were dragged into prison just as the bird, which is a kind of metaphor for the free world, is captured too. It is a shocking image, but it is a real pity to take it out.'[117] At the same time a similar problem arose for the Mexican director Alejandro Iñárritu, whose dogfighting scenes in his film *Amores Perros* (2000) caused such controversy. For him the humane message of the film is dependent on such imagery being shown. In these instances the violence perpetrated on animal and human bodies should not necessarily be seen differently. Iñárritu found the controversy misguided both because the fights were carefully faked and because of the hypocrisy involved in the critique: 'The dogs were treated better than the actors. People ignore a young guy dying of AIDS in the street, but they see a cat with a drop of blood and they go "Oh, poor cat!" I saw *Gladiator* on the plane. They cut off heads but that's considered OK.'[118] Implicit in this argument are two different humane projects. The first is characterized by the metaphorical parallels that seek to collapse human and animal at some level and which highlight a shared experience of suffering. The second detaches human and animal suffering as separate issues, but also bases itself on a refusal to read the animal image purely as an image.

This split within the animal image – the artificial image that never can quite be read as artificial – is one that ruptures all readings of it.

3 animal life and death

Gregg Mitman follows a well-worn critical path when he points out that the objectification of the animal in film, largely for entertainment purposes, substitutes seeing for the experiences of contact or labour with animals, which, in turn, reinforces a sense of separation.[1] However, at the same time, as he himself admits, animal films were a powerful inspiration for him to become more deeply involved in the study of the animal kingdom. It is important to recognize this transformative potential of the animal film, as a counterbalance to analyses that restrict themselves to the implications of the objectification of the animal (both as truth-telling and as a process of detachment and domination). It reminds us that the ethical potential of animal films cannot necessarily be mapped onto their truth value. There is, in other words, constant vacillation between the relative advantages and disadvantages of detachment from or attachment to animals.

These two, often contradictory, ways of looking at animal films stem from a tension within the animal image itself. This is a tension between their depiction of the 'authentic' and the values of feeling and entertainment. As we have seen, it is a polarization that over time has structured a great deal of writing on animal films. Even notions of authenticity are problematized because of the sense that the naturalness of the animal is always going to be corrupted in the process of becoming an image. Compared to such a standard of 'naturalness', understood here as a special quality of the animal, any form of representation will be either a fiction or in some way falsely motivated. Hence the common tropes of nature film criticism: violence is sensationalism; sentimentality is contrived; narratives, if not anthropomorphized, are subject to simplification; and the glorious visual aesthetics of blue-chip nature documentaries are romanticizations. This makes it difficult to decide how animals ought to be represented, if at all. Critical descriptions of a popularized fascination with animals, which is seen as compromising the need for greater objectivity, often underestimate the extent of amateur knowledge of natural history and popular involvement in animal-related societies and activities, as well as the level of public engagement with environmental issues. Furthermore, the contrast between the disciplined gaze of the scientist or expert and the voyeuristic gaze of the public is itself undermined by the capacity for sadism in the eye of the scientist. Overall, however, these complicated dilemmas cannot but be subsumed under a broader general pessimism with regard to the future of animals, as well as humans, on the planet. As Alexander Wilson remarks, wildlife movies are 'documents of a culture trying to come to terms with . . . "the end of nature.'"[2] The notion of the corrupt image signals, in effect, another version of the Fall. Yet, keeping with the religious tone of this idea, we might say that the image can also be presented as a means of redemption.

The tradition of using film to make points about animal welfare has a long history and some of the early examples are quite striking. In 1914 *The Times* carried a story concerning an RSPCA film made to address the question of decrepit horse traffic.[3]

> The pictures as shown privately yesterday are never likely to be displayed before the general public, for, deeply impressive as they are, no censor would pass them for general exhibition, and no cinematograph theatre manager would put them into an ordinary programme. The earlier pictures show the arrival of the animals and their weary progress through the streets, and to these, pathetic as they are, no objection could be taken. But in the closing stages, by way of an argument in favour of a humane killer, the film shows a primitive method of slaughtering the unfortunate beasts by driving a knife into the chest. As the blood surges out the animal's death struggles are seen with repulsive realism. The Society itself admits that these pictures cannot be shown in public, however vividly they prove the need for some improvement of existing conditions.

Another early example was a film made by the Council of Justice to Animals and the Humane Slaughter Association in the mid-1920s, which concerned efforts to introduce humane killers, in this case a captive bolt gun, into slaughter-houses, so that animals were properly rendered unconscious or killed before being bled. The film first shows a series of animals (a pig, a sheep and a calf) killed without prior stunning, followed by the same series of animals being slaughtered using the humane method. In the first sequence of killing the graphic footage is further dramatized when a pig is stuck while still standing, rather than being hoisted on a chain, and rolls around in its death throes until it is completely covered in its own blood.

In the light of the extensive use of photography and film in animal politics we can assume that the visual image is as significant to the history of these debates as the ideas and texts from which historians more usually derive them. It is usually argued that the exploitation of visual imagery for the purposes of animal rights is due to the fact that animals cannot speak up for themselves, so the message is in greater need of visual reinforcement than, presumably, for issues of human rights. In fact, the actual power of this imagery derives from a much longer term concern over public codes concerning what should and should not be seen.[4] Deborah Blum points to the parallels between a break-in at a laboratory in the United States in the 1920s, in which people brought out photographs of dogs with their mouths taped shut, and Alex Pacheco's secret photography of abuse of primates at the Silver Spring laboratory, so crucial to the rise of People for the Ethical Treatment of Animals (PETA).[5] The eruption of this kind of imagery, making the hidden visible, has far-reaching effects in the public domain. In Britain a landmark event in animal rights was the publication, in early 1975, of a photograph taken secretly by a *Sunday People* journalist of beagles being made to smoke cigarettes in a laboratory. This caused a considerable public outcry leading to a debate in the House of Commons and the closing of the experiment.[6] One might also note that the animal protest that has probably had the highest media profile for the longest period of time has concerned the very visible practice of fox-hunting, often at the expense of less conspicuous welfare questions such as factory farming.

More famously, the world of film and animal issues came together in the iconic 1977 picture of Brigitte Bardot and a baby seal in the protest against seal clubbing in Canada. In her interesting critique of the imagery of this protest as

Brigitte Bardot's famous protest against seal clubbing in Canada, 1977.

overdetermined by both erotic and colonial factors, Chantal
Nadeau draws attention to the historical precedents to which
this action can be related. This photograph represented a
translation of the liberal bourgeois tradition in Europe and
the United States of 'wealthy women's involvement in char-
ity works' into the world of celebrity and movie stars.[7] The
cultivation of high-profile celebrity support by animal
organizations today, especially PETA, echoes the extensive
aristocratic and upper-middle class patronage for animal
causes in the late-nineteenth and early-twentieth century.
Particularly relevant here is the campaign in Britain against
plumage in ladies' fashions, 'murderous millinery' as some
termed it, conducted mainly by women activists of
respectable social standing. Among the significant consequences of the campaign were the creation of the Society of
the Protection of Birds in 1893 and the passing of the Anti-
Plumage Act in 1927. This particular link between animal
welfare and visible display again has a modern parallel in
campaigns against the wearing of fur, strikingly illustrated by
David Bailey's advertisement in which models walked down a
catwalk in fur coats that, as the models turned, sprayed the
audience with blood. There may be a difference in scale
between the fin-de-siècle and nowadays – the pamphleteers
and letter writers of 100 years ago did not initially have the
benefits of film – but the importance of issues of visibility, as
regards the treatment of animals, and the cultivation of aristocratic, or nowadays celebrity, support are closely inter-
linked. This is not to say that the good works they are seen to

do are not genuinely ethical, yet they are still very much focussed on visible surfaces.

Many of the films and video tapes that are produced in the name of animal rights are, despite the roughness of the camerawork and the grainy imagery, still subject to the common tropes of animal cinematography. For example, films using hidden cameras uncannily echo the secret filming of wildlife from hides; the editing process often gives us a carefully selected montage of the most horrific sequences reminiscent of the way in which violent animal imagery is edited from longer footage; a *cinéma-vérité* or 'fly-on-the-wall' documentary effect is frequently gained from the hand-held camerawork. The lack of aesthetic refinement in the image mirrors both the abject nature of the subject matter and the manner in which any sense of humanity has been stripped from the footage of the behaviour shown towards the depicted animals. Thus, the Born Free Foundation's video entitled *Mentally Damaged Animals in Captivity* is mainly a collection of roughly shot sequences, taken from zoos all over the world, of animals showing repetitive movements in inadequate caging.[8] One of the most disconcerting of many such sequences in this film is of a gorilla vomiting and then eating the vomit. This imagery is also intercut with scientific commentary to lend it authority. Similarly, in PETA's video *Dog Lab*, a short film of a dog being vivisected as part of medical students' training, the film includes comments by surgeons observing various failings in the procedure. Interestingly, this film is also framed at the beginning and the end by

shots of dogs in cages to remind us that the dogs being operated upon come from the local pound. This plays on a point
made throughout the history of the anti-vivisection debate,
which is that the procedure threatens, at one remove, the pets
in the family home. The commentary in these films echo the
techniques of documentary, whilst the horrific nature of the
imagery suggests that the examples presented offer a self-
evident moral truth.[9] As Jasper and Paulson put it in a study
that compares animal rights and anti-nuclear protest, 'the
visual images used in animal rights recruitment have a simple
but effective structure based on good versus evil.'[10]

A wide range of issues appear under the umbrella title
of 'animal welfare', or the more politically charged term
'animal rights', not all of which are necessarily constituted by
the same kinds of arguments, except at the most general level.
Although these issues turn on the basic question of what is
humane or inhumane, they cut across a variety of dissimilar
practices from, for instance, fox-hunting to zoos, scientific
experimentation to whale hunting, pet-keeping to conservation. Visual imagery of mistreatment is one way of binding
them together. This reduces the complexity of these various
practices to a basic question of impact on the animal body
whilst, at the same time, presenting a montage effect of similarly striking images (the dead fox, the slaughtered whale, the
laboratory animal). These are often amalgamated, particularly
in television documentaries, to define the boundaries of
animal politics in terms of a form of visual similarity.[11] Structurally, there is nothing in this that differs from the practice of

using striking animal imagery to sell other kinds of nature film. Mitman gives a good example of this when he cites how Time-Life Video advertised the David Attenborough film series, *Trials of Life* (1991), by condensing all the animal attack sequences into one sequence, much to Attenborough's horror.[12] Thus, there may be, as Jasper and Paulson note, a self-evident moral truth to animal rights imagery, but such imagery is still highly troped.

In the mid-1970s the American documentary maker Frederick Wiseman made two important films on animals: *Primate* (1974), which was filmed at the Yerkes Research Center in Atlanta, and *Meat* (1976), which followed the processing, or 'fabrication' as the plant owner put it, of animals at a meat-packing plant from arrival to packaging. Both films contain plenty of potentially disconcerting imagery. In *Primate* there is a long dissection sequence, for instance. In these films, little is explained and much is seen. Unlike the makers of animal welfare films Wiseman has said that he has no strong opinions on animal research or meat-eating.[13] The dispassionate camera in the slaughterhouse simply reflects the mechanical nature of the overall process being shown. However, it also echoes the static aesthetic frame of the much more political Humane Slaughter Association film discussed earlier, in which everything took place in front of an open doorway with carcasses in the room beyond. In fact, both films have a certain neat symmetry as shown by the sequence of animal killings in the HSA film (pig-sheep-calf-sheep-pig) and the way that in Wiseman's film the second half repeats the first except that it focuses on sheep rather than cattle; the combination of repetitive slaughter and mechanical organization is implicit in the very structure. Whereas many PETA videos are relatively short, making their point quickly but with great intensity, their video, *A Day in the Life of a Massachusetts Slaughterhouse*, lasts some 90 minutes. There is no particular plot structure to the film as the camera observes a succession of animals being processed in a small abattoir. In this case, there is also no commentary. Apart from one brief outdoor shot of animals in a field, the whole film is taken up with the business of killing and butchery. As an anti-meat film the case could have been made fairly quickly, but the film runs at length which has the effect, intentionally or otherwise, of reinforcing the implications consequent upon this being an industrial process. Industrial slaughter is repetitive, a fact that can also be seen in Tim Macmillan's video loop (1998) repeating the image of a horse at the moment of being killed in an abattoir.

The imagery of mechanization and anonymity appears interchangeably whether in art film, documentary or animal rights videos on the meat process. One might almost call it a slaughterhouse aesthetic. Jane Giles, in an article on butchery and film, considers such imagery sadistic: 'material documenting the torture and murder of animals seems to provide a stop-gap for the hungry sadistic eye'.[14] In this sense, the sadism would lie in the dispassionate camera in the abattoir, regardless of the sympathies of the filmmakers. But there is another important aspect to these kinds of films. The fetishization of animal death as part of an industrial process renders visible that which we rarely, if ever, see. Few films, however, actually explore the relationship between this revelatory imagery and other aspects of culture, preferring instead to reinforce its sense of separateness. Magnetized as the eye might be to the act of animal killing, whether through fascination, repulsion or a combination of the two, the sense of isolation that the act has behind the walls of the abattoir is in fact reinforced.

Franju's *Sang des bêtes*, made in 1949, is an exception to this rule. Although it was filmed in a different era, one in which the slaughter process was less mechanized, the images it depicts are not so dissimilar from the films discussed above. The film weaves imagery of Paris, particularly its transport networks, with footage of the work of slaughter. The symbolic associations between the canals of Paris and the rivers of blood in the abattoirs – the city as historically a site of violence – are easy to make. The commentary, written by Jean Painlevé, is spoken by a female voice, Nicole Ladmiral, when referring to the city, and by a male voice, Georges Hubert, when dealing with the slaughter itself. Despite the networks of trains and canals linking the city with the world outside that provide the animals, an interrelated system that works with great efficiency, the city is, like the bodies of its beasts, fragmented. At the beginning of the film various forms of bric-à-brac litter the waste grounds that lie beside the slums and the railway tracks entering the city. In one shot an armless mannequin, a gramophone horn and a basket combine in an almost surreal figure: 'jumbled delights for the curio seeker [*Tout un bonheur désassorti s'offre aux amateurs de brocante*], for poets and passing lovers, at the edge of the domain of trucks and trains'.[15] This anticipates a later shot in which a discarded foetus lies on the floor of the abattoir next to various piles of innards.

Franju's film is particularly rich because of the number of registers on which it plays. Alongside the horror of the killing and the efficiency of the networks that enable it, the treatment of the abattoir workers is sympathetic. In the tension between images of networks and fragmentation, we can read the idea that the animal is essential to the dynamics of the city, a city that is ultimately built upon broken bodies. If killing is always at some level ritualistic, these are the sacrifices that enable societies to function. What Franju's film makes visible is the extent to which the systems of modernity are built around the figure of the animal. Although Franju certainly intended to shock, he does not quite evoke that peculiar combination of detachment and horror that characterizes the other films I have mentioned.[16] As Franju put it, 'violence is not an end, it's a weapon which sensitizes the spectator and which lets him see what's lyric or poetic beyond or above the violence, or what's tender in reality.'[17] In other words, by moving between the invisible practice of slaughter and the highly visible city, his film follows a more transgressive course by making killing more than merely a confined act. I would say that his less 'sadistic eye' reveals a far greater and more pervasive sadism.

In contrast to the moral dynamics that can be located in images of animal death, it might appear that the opposite impulse, the celebration of the living animal, would produce a different set of associations, one less linked to the brutalistic networks of modernity. I have in mind the emotional simplicity of sentimental family films or the pure delights that can be had from a nature documentary. But, in fact, even here human–animal relations are closely linked to issues of loss. I am not thinking of the death of pets or the extinction of species, but rather of the place of the animal in larger types of networks: the ways in which the animal may be situated at junctures of emotional attachment and kinship networks, or visual aesthetics and narrative structures.[18] Franju juxtaposes the killing of animals with the networks of Paris. Just as the blood of dead animals animates the city, so too the living animal in film animates the links between humans, participates in networks, and even creates relations that previously did not exist. In family films featuring animals, for example, one of the most common motifs concerns the missing or dead parent and the manner in which animals come to heal or in some ways compensate for that absence. Given the sentimentalism of many of these films, one could say that this is a version of the orphan or step-parent motifs found in folk and fairy tales. Bousé has identified the orphan theme, along with other structures like cyclical plots and journeys, as the classic model for most animal narratives and this model is usually structured as a rite of passage formula involving a process of separation, initiation and return.[19] However, I want to take his idea a little further and suggest that it also has to do with the fractured nature of the animal image and what is ultimately an arbitrariness in its connection with humans.

Alejandro Iñárritu's triptych of stories in *Amores Perros* (2000) explores the causes and consequences of a car accident for a number of different people involved and is threaded together by the significance of the relations between dogs and humans on the one hand, and missing fathers on the other. At one level, in keeping with the idea that pets can indeed be substitutes for things lacking in human relations, the dogs can be seen as symbolic. In the first story, the fighting dogs reflect, amongst other things, the aggressive conflict between two brothers, Octavio and Ramiro; in the second story, the pet dog trapped under the floor of the flat reflects the helplessness of the woman model, Valeria, crippled in the accident; and in the third story, the fighting dog destroys all the other pet dogs of the ex-guerrilla, El Chivo ('the goat' in Spanish), just as his own decision to leave his family for the revolutionary cause has laid waste to their lives as well as his own. There is nothing subtle or concealed about this metaphorical interplay and it works to good effect. But the other dimension of the film lies in the manner in which the dogs actively transform the situations of those about them. The dog fights give Octavio the possibility of rising above his situation and replacing his brother who is, incidentally, a husband and father. In the second story the dog trapped under the floor intensifies the misery and loss of the man who has left his wife and family for Valeria who, as soon as they start their new life together, loses her legs in the car accident. It is the dog that truly catalyses the sense of despair that their situation brings. At the end of the final story, El Chivo, the father, leaves a message of apology and love for his now grown-up daughter, whose life he has never been part of, on her answerphone. Having discarded his appearance of shabby tramp for that of the middle-aged academic he would probably have become, he sets off across a desolate wasteland accompanied by the fighting dog, Cofi. There is some sense of redemption to this ending in that he can move on having finally sloughed off some of his past. But the cycles of violence throughout the film, as reflected by the figure of the dog fight, provide an ambivalent message. Whilst the violence might be cathartic in the sense of creating the possibility of freedom, the characters remain trapped in their situations. The motifs of inadequate communication that recur in the film – anonymous phone calls, particularly in the second story, and the answerphone message at the end – seem appropriate in a film in which dogs *say* so much. It might seem that neither the dog nor the telephone can redeem all these fragmented relationships. Yet, paradoxically, the final shot of the film suggests that, in the bleakest of landscapes, the bond between man and dog will enable other kinds of transformations in the future.

There is a complex interplay between the emotive simplicity of the animal image, the manner in which it appeals to sentiment and feeling, and its potential for overdetermination at the level of meaning. In *Amores Perros*, I have only mentioned a few of the many themes in the film and one could go on to explore all sorts of other dimensions through the figure of the dog, such as gender or issues within Mexican politics. However, it is important to avoid the conclusion that this multiplicity is the end of the story, the idea that the animal is a *tabula rasa*, as mentioned earlier in the book. An emotional response to the animal image is in fact integral to its semantics and, rather like the multiplicity of meanings an animal can carry, points to a fractured rather than cohesive view of the animal image. The transformative potential of the animal is one demonstration of this and it gives the animal the role of something like a transitional object. But, as in *Amores Perros*, those transitions that are enabled by the animal do not always lead to any form of resolution, even if they set human relations on a new and different path.

In the Walt Disney film *Old Yeller* (1957), set in Texas in the 1860s, a father leaves his eldest son, Travis, to look after farm and family while he goes on a cattle drive. Travis most desires a horse and the father promises him one on his return. The film is a rite of passage story in which the boy comes of age during his father's absence. Yeller, a golden Labrador from another farm, becomes part of the family and changes from being an untrustworthy thieving dog to faithful pet. Near the end of the film, Yeller defends the family against an attack by a wolf but contracts rabies and is again transformed, this time into a vicious dog foaming at the mouth. Travis has to shoot him. Although the film has many of the motifs of resolution and renewal typical of family films in which animals are killed – most commonly with the subsequent arrival of newborns – the sense of trauma is not truly overcome. *Old Yeller* is different from many family films in which animals, if they die at all, are usually killed through accident, hunting or illness. Rarely does a child have to kill their own pet, whom they love more than anything. Travis buries Yeller under a cairn on a hill overlooking the farm, a perpetual reminder of a loss not quite compensated for by his father's pride in his son's manliness: 'Mighty proud of how my boy stood up to it. Couldn't ask no more of a grown man. Thing to do now is try and forget it, go on being a man.' Were it not for the visible reminder of the cairn, Travis's acceptance of a new Labrador pup at the end of the film would seem to suggest that the trauma of leaving adolescence could in some sense be forgotten. But the tension between the highly idealized and sentimental depiction of a family and the moment of the killing cuts right through the film. Taken together, they indicate that the renewal consequent on animal death is not one that entails a simple moving on. The sacrifice necessary for the rite of passage requires its scar.

There are two important and well-known family films made after *Old Yeller* in which loss is also central: *Born Free* (1966) and *Ring of Bright Water* (1969). Both these films starred the husband and wife team, Bill Travers and Virginia McKenna, who later became involved in animal protection, especially in relation to zoos. Both films were based on autobiographical writings, by Joy Adamson and Gavin Maxwell respectively. In *Born Free* the lioness Elsa is orphaned when her parents are shot by gamewardens and she is brought up as a surrogate child, who then has to be re-released into the wild. This is partly due to the fact that she is ready to have cubs and partly because she has become a local nuisance. The attempts to abandon Elsa in the wild are some of the most poignant moments of the film. At the very end the Adamsons' sense of loss is redeemed by the reappearance of Elsa with a litter of cubs. However, they resist the temptation to handle the cubs or treat them as pets in order to preserve their wildness. (In the sequel *Living Free* (1972), made by a different team, Elsa dies and the Adamsons have to catch her three cubs and get them to a new home in the Serengeti.) There are some similarities in narrative structure of *Ring of Bright Water*. An aspiring writer buys an otter as a pet and leaves London to live in an isolated cottage on the Scottish coast. The pet otter, Mij, is accidentally killed, though again a mother otter with her pups, presumably fathered by Mij, appears at the end. It is the loss of the otter that enables the writer to find the ability to write. In both these stories it is difficult to decide whether the redemptive endings really make up for the loss or whether the loss permeates the whole cycle of the narrative. After all, Mij's pups will be fatherless.

Interestingly, in these two films the themes of loss and redemption spilled over into real life. The filming of *Born Free* had an important impact on McKenna and Travers. The two actors had made it a condition of their contract before filming that no doubles would play their scenes with the lions and, while the film crew worked from within wire cages, they

Filming *Roar* (Noel Marshall, 1981).

One of the tigers at the Shambala Preserve animal sanctuary, Acton, CA.

themselves worked outside with the lions. The process was not without its accidents, but they wanted to be as close to the lions as possible and worked hard with George Adamson on getting to know the individual quirks of all the lions on set.[20] Virginia McKenna later wrote,

In retrospect we see that *Born Free* was not an end in itself, as we probably thought at the time – we believed then that the incredible experience of working with lions in the particular way we did, and our close contact with nature, was a crystallization of a myriad of our half-conscious thoughts and feelings and longings . . . We could never be the same again.[21]

A similar story of an acting family transformed by their contact with lions is that of Tippi Hedren, who starred in Alfred Hitchcock's *The Birds* (1963), and Noel Marshall's making of the film *Roar*. Hedren and Marshall had founded a lion preserve in California, which they used for making an animal movie set in Africa. Previous to this they had already kept lions at their home. The undertaking became considerably large-scale. When they began filming in October 1976 (the film would take three years to make) their collection included 132 lions, tigers, leopards, cougars and jaguars, and one elephant.[22] As in the *Born Free* story, the lion reflected a sometimes unstable combination of wildness, the enterprise was not without its accidents, and affection, since many of the lions owned by Hedren and Marshall were effectively an extension of their family. As films like *Born Free* and *Old Yeller* indicate, the figure of the animal opens up the experience of humans to a richer life whilst at the same time making this experience dependent on some form of absence and loss.

In general, however, films of this kind promote a much simpler version of the happy ending. *Free Willy* has the orphan Jesse coming to terms with his status as a foster child. In the next film, *Free Willy 2* (1995), Jesse finds he has a half-brother whom he initially hates, but the ordeal of rescuing whales brings the two together, as well as enabling him to come to terms with his mother's death. There are plenty of similar examples. The remake of *The Incredible Journey* (1963), entitled *Homeward Bound: The Incredible Journey* (1993), also sees the reuniting of family and animals at the end of the film, which in turn cements the children's relationship with their new stepfather. Comparable motifs also crop up in films like *Flipper* (1996); *Fly Away Home* (1996), in which a girl loses her mother and goes to live with her eccentric father; and *Fluke* (1995), where the father who is killed in a car accident is reincarnated as a dog. In a recent version of *Lassie* (1994), the dog, who has lost his owner in a lorry crash, attaches himself to another family and enables the boy, Matt, to overcome the death of his mother and reconcile himself to life in the countryside with his father and stepmother. The recent French film *La Vache et le Président* (1999) also brings human and animal together round the theme of missing parents. Here, a cow dies giving birth just as the boy's own mother died giving birth to him. When the new cow, Maeva, who the boy takes on as his own, is threatened with slaughter due to the possibility of having BSE, the subsequent adventures result both in a reprieve for the cow and a new partner for his father. An adult version of this theme can be found in the positive impact of a dog on the relations between a misanthropic and homophobic writer, Verdell, and his gay dog-owning neighbour, Simon, in *As Good As It Gets* (1997), a film that begins with Verdell attempting to dispose of the dog down the laundry shoot.

The motif of the incomplete family also ran through many animal television series made in the United States during the 1950s and '60s, most of which were either inspired by or followed on from animal films. The sequel to the original *Flipper* film (1963), *Flipper's New Adventure*, as well as the follow-up television series features the lead, Porter Ricks, as a widower. The family for the first television series of *Lassie* featured a widowed mother, and in the second series the family was made up of an orphan, a childless couple and the orphan's uncle. Similar motifs occur in *Champion*, the story of the relationship between a wild horse and a young boy who lives with his uncle, and *Fury*, a series in which a widower runs a ranch and becomes foster father to a boy from the city.[23] Ivan Tors, the producer of the *Flipper* films, once told a *TV Guide* reporter that, 'the father image in the United States is in dreadful shape. A stronger image is needed and we provide it.'[24] Although the implication of such films is that animals make up for the loss in human relations, there is a darker side that accompanies this sentimentalized and therapeutic ideology.[25] The climax of *La Vache et le Président* involves a race against time to save Maeva, when it is discovered that she is free of BSE, just as she is sent down to the slaughterhouse to be destroyed. The cow follows a path through the sterile environment of the abattoir, all gleaming white and polished steel, down to the restraining device where she will be killed. Although Maeva is saved, the film does depict the nature of the fate of all the other cows. The caricaturized developers who seek to destroy a natural habitat for migrant birds as in *Fly Away Home*, or the dolphin-murdering polluters in *Flipper*, suggest that, even in family films, some form of shadow, however faint, must be cast over all happy endings. These kinds of plots may be trivializing or at best benign but they still lock into the moral imperatives that govern all animal imagery. Death or divorce in the family is, after all, a threat to family cohesion, rupturing the 'natural' ties of child and parent, just as nature is threatened by various forms of development. These films have a similar moral purpose to sentimental instructional tales for children with regard to outlining how one should behave and the manner in which animal and human relations are supposed to mirror each other. Children who are recalcitrant or unhappy at the beginning of these films, often because of some family trauma, are transformed by the end through their contact with animals.

Criticisms of these family films have often been made on the grounds that their sentimentalism and anthropomorphism create a comfortable complacency in attitudes to animals. However, what kinds of imagery would it be more appropriate for children to see? And what kind of imagery would be more *true* to the position of animals in the world? A further implication of this critique of family films is that the moral messages so evident in these films, especially those that seem to be defining appropriate conduct for others, are taking an inappropriate form. I noted in the first chapter an asceticism that runs through certain theories about the position of animals in culture which, as I have noted, has its roots in the idea that the animal as a natural non-human object is always automatically corrupted or falsified as soon as it is troped by visual imagery. But the issue here is not really the mollifying of human consciences via sentimentalism. Rather it concerns whether or not animal films should entail or inspire a sense of the real animal uncluttered by the emotional and psychological links that allow for human–animal relations in the first place. The visual animal is caught in an argument over whether the animal should be considered on its own terms or understood through a network of human–animal relations. As an aside it is unlikely that one would come across criticism of a human sentimental comedy on the grounds that it might make one complacent in one's attitude to other humans because life is never that funny anyway.

Given that our culture is saturated with animal imagery of all kinds, and given the diversity of the audiences that receive it, it is difficult to assess what particular kinds of animal imagery feed the different attitudes and actions we take towards the animal world. Admittedly, when audiences do respond to the plight of animals as a result of a film this response can be highly selective and unpredictable. The extraordinary public financial response to, and interest in, the plight of Keiko, the whale in *Free Willy*, who was being kept in a theme park in Mexico, is a case in point.[26] There are also films that have led to an surge in sales of featured animals.

This happened, for instance, with kestrels after *Kes* (1969) was released. In an interesting development of this, a film-maker recently provided the public with guidelines as to whether or not to buy an animal after seeing a film. Included in the titles at the end of *102 Dalmations* is the caveat that 'the producers, the Walt Disney Company, the American Humane Association and the Dalmatian Club of America want every pet to have a loving and permanent home. If you are adopting a pet be sure you are ready for a lifetime commitment and research your choice carefully.' The advice is sensible but coming after two films – *101 Dalmations* (1996) and *102 Dalmations* (2000) – that have effectively acted as advertisements for this visually striking breed of dogs, it seems an inadequate gesture.

Bleaker films with greater realism, in which the links between human and animal are set against a more pessimistic background, do not necessarily mean that the attachments between human and animal carry less transformative potential. Indeed, many of the narrative motifs are similar to those described above in sentimental family films. Examples such as *Kes*, the Iranian Kurdish film *A Time for Drunken Horses* (2000), the Japanese film *The Eel* (1997) and, though slightly different, Bresson's *Au hazard Balthazar* (1966), may be more serious and unsentimental but still suggest that the parameters of human–animal relations are premised on interlocking themes of loss and the possibility of change.[27]

In *Kes* a boy, Billy Casper, lives with his bullying brother and mother on an estate in a mining town. Another boy without a father, he finds and trains a kestrel that provides, temporarily, an escape from the life in which he is trapped. In *A Time for Drunken Horses*, Ayoub, a young Iranian Kurd who has lost his parents, takes over responsibility for his family. In order to try and get money for an operation for his crippled brother, Madi, he joins the smuggling bands with their horses going up the mountains into Iraq. The title of the film is taken from the fact that the horses are given alcohol to enable them to cope on the cold arduous journeys. A different version of loss appears in *The Eel*. A man comes home to find

Barry Hines and David Bradley (Billy Casper) with two of the three falcons used in the making of *Kes* (Ken Loach, 1969).

his wife committing adultery and kills her. On leaving prison with the eel he has kept as a pet, he starts up a barbershop, confiding his thoughts to the eel as, with difficulty, he becomes increasingly involved with the world around him. In *Au hazard Balthazar* these themes are inverted in that it is the animal, an ass named Balthazar, rather than the human that is at the centre of the film, enduring a succession of owners and trials. The film plays on the dual nature of the ass as both saintly, the holy animal that bears Christ into Jerusalem, and worthless, a beast of burden, subject to all sorts of indignities.[28] Like Balthazar, all the animals in these films are fractured images; they do not reflect a symbolic unity. As Ken Loach remarked with regard to *Kes*, 'we never thought of the kestrel as a symbol. I don't think we ever once discussed the symbolic resonance of it – again tending and training the bird was just what Billy did.'[29] However, the kestrel, like the lions discussed earlier, is both half-tame and half-wild. The eel is also out of place living in a bare fish tank and doing nothing. The mules in the Iranian film stagger drunkenly under their burdens while being at the same time the means of salvation for Ayoub and Madi. The recognizable animal tropes in these films mean that it is important not to equate sentimentality with a lack of reality or bleakness with realism. The structures of human–animal relations shape both these styles, particularly in relation to the shared themes of loss.

In experimental filmmaking, a body of work whose diversity is not easy to summarize, these issue of connectivity and loss are not in play in the same way as in other genres of film, which link the animal more closely to the kinds of narratives and cultural structures I have been discussing. However, the fragmentary and dislocated form that the animal imagery takes in experimental or avant-garde film does refer to such issues, even if in a different register. The London contemporary film institution Lux assembled, in 1998, a series of films under the title 'Animal Magic'. This collection contains an intriguing mix of technological manipulation and animation. Taken on its own the animal imagery could best be described as stripped of cultural connotations were it not for the manner in which the techniques of this filmmaking organize the animal in familiar ways. Technology's exploration of outward visual surfaces can make sense of the links between human and animal by delineating a visual field that itself works as the main force of connection, even if the links seem arbitrary, alienating and full of odd juxtapositions. In fact, the ordinariness of the animal image in such films and, to my eyes, a certain backward looking feel when considered in the context of the whole tradition of animal film imagery, suggest again that characteristic interplay of the archaic and the modern I have outlined above. Just as with Bill Viola's collage of different styles in his video film *I Do Not Know What It Is I Am Like*, these experimental films exploit technology in ways we are familiar with from other forms of animal filmmaking. For example, Sam Easterson's *A Sheep in Wolf's Clothing* (1997), in which a video camera is attached to the head of a sheep that then runs around a field; the slow motion or repeated loops of the leaping lemur in *Animal Charms* (1998), *Stuffing* (1997) or the cows in

Experimental animal imagery: two stills from George S. Best's *Untitled (Pigeons)*, 1997.

Hermut Jahn's *Concert in Muh* (1997); the time-lapse sequences of pigeons slowly forming a square in George S. Best's *Untitled* (1997); or Pieter Baan Müller's *Scouting the Backyard*, in which he follows a duck round his courtyard that then flies off. Other films involve mixtures of animation and live footage, strange coloured microscopic organisms, and painting or sticking organisms directly onto the film-strip, such as in Stan Brakhage's *Mothlight* (1963).[30] If anything these films point even further back in time to things like the repeating movements of animals in Muybridge's Zoopraxiscope, the films of Percy Smith, early hand-tinting, and again the long tradition of trick nature photography. In these contemporary films the animal image is fragmented so that on the one hand the issue of loss surfaces through the play of technique while, on the other hand, the ordinariness of much of the imagery seems to repair it.

Jean Painlevé, the French filmmaker who made many beautiful and often bizarre nature films, particularly of sea creatures, saw cinema as a synthesis of art, poetry and science. His short documentary film of a vampire bat (1945), which combined imagery from Murnau's *Nosferatu* with shots of the bat feasting on a guinea pig accompanied by the music of Duke Ellington, was described by Bazin as both a 'zoological document and the fulfillment of the great sanguinary mythology'.[31] But the strands of science, art and myth that are brought together around the animal figure here are more juxtaposed than synthesized, working in tension with the idea that the animal might be a figure of resolution. As Painlevé

Jean Painlevé with
camera, c. 1935.

wrote about his film *The Sea Horse* (1934), 'the seahorse was
for me a splendid way of promoting the kindness and virtue of
the father while at the same time underlining the necessity of
the mother. In other words I wanted to reestablish the balance
between male and female.'[32] But, the sense of loss and frac-
ture that the animal image also brings with it haunts this resolution. It seems no coincidence that Painlevé's artistic roots
were in Surrealism. Surrealism cultivated the randomness
and strangeness that so often characterize animal film. We
might think of the donkeys in the pianos in Buñuel's *Un chien
andalou* (1928), stuffed as they were with rotting fish by Dalí,
their eyes oozing wax. Here again we find, as so often
throughout the history of film, an animal is present at a semi-
nal moment in the history of cinema, although in this instance

it is hidden in the infamous sequence of the cutting of the eye with the razor blade.[33] In *Un chien andalou* Buñuel used the eye of a calf.

In his remarks on Alfred Hitchcock's *The Birds* Donald Spoto notes that the characters say 'I see' or 'You see' over 40 times. He writes, 'the words are like a refrain, punctuating every stanza of his cinematic poem, just as every sequence ends with a dissolve of a character staring into space.'[34] The closing shots of the film where the panoptic birds finally observe the departure of the (fatherless) 'family' group seems to me one of the most striking examples in which the looks between human and animal reshape the orders of society and nature. Because I am an animal historian who has become interested in film (rather than a film historian who has become interested in animals) I have been drawn to account for how animal imagery directs our attention to the history of human–animal relations in modernity. But I have also taken it as read that animals on film have a powerful and formative impact on this history. There is no doubt that the animal is a key figure in the history of filmmaking though, curiously, it is a fact that has been virtually ignored until recently. Film also tells us a great deal about the animal at that meeting point of technology and the value systems that frame the animal. These two poles constantly interact on each other. The sophistication with which film explores the question of looking and the manner in which the strands of communication, trauma, ethics and technology are woven round the visual seem to me to point as much in positive directions as negative ones. I am aware that I have taken only a fraction of the possible examples that could be discussed in this field. Paietta and Kaupilla's filmography of *Animals on Screen and Radio* lists nearly 1,500 film and television series and does not include many more serious and relevant films such as Peter Greenaway's *A Zed and Two Noughts* (1985) or Lasse Hallström's *My Life as a Dog* (1985) to name but two. (Both, incidentally, also turn on issues of looking and loss.) However, it seems to me that much of what I have written is applicable to a very broad range of animal films, or films that feature animal motifs. What I have attempted in this book is to outline a field of research whereby considerations of the history of animals on film are not divorced from wider and more general considerations of the history of animals. Nor need the details of plot be divorced from these issues either. In fact, this book has sought to bind together the fragments that up to now have constituted the history of the film animal and, as far as possible, to cast a positive slant on the loss that previous theories have reinforced.

Tiger being filmed against a blue screen.

references

prologue

1 *The Times*, 31 October 1949, p. 5.
2 On the cultural construction of animals in relation to the foxhunt, see Garry Marvin, 'Cultured Killers: Creating and Representing Foxhounds', *Society and Animals*, IX (2001), pp. 273–92.
3 Michael Powell, *Million-Dollar Man* (London, 1992), pp. 71–2.
4 See Matt Cartmell, *A View to a Death in the Morning: Hunting and Nature through History* (Cambridge, MA, 1993), p. 178.
5 Judith Brennan, 'The Pets of Prime Time', *Emmy*, XIX (1997), p. 31.
6 Anne Thompson, 'Bear with Us', *Film Comment*, XXV (1989), pp. 2 and 4.

1 film and the history of the visual animal

1 Derek Bousé, *Wildlife Films* (Philadelphia, 2000); Gregg Mitman, *Reel Nature: America's Romance with Wildlife on Film* (Cambridge, MA, 1999). These two books have been key texts for my research and my debt to them both is considerable. However, I have tried to avoid reproducing too much of the material that they discuss so

well. Although there are wildlife film festivals and conferences, there have been few devoted to animal films in general. One exception was an interesting programme of animal films put together by Geoff Andrew for a season in 1987; *National Film Theatre Programme* (December 1987), p. 3.

2 Raymond Lee, *Not So Dumb: The Life and Times of the Animal Actors* (Cranbury, NJ, 1970), p. 106.

3 See my article 'Violent Health and the Moving Image: The London Zoo and Monkey Hill' in Mary Henninger-Voss, ed., *Animals in Human Histories: The Mirror of Nature and Culture* (Rochester, NY, 2002).

4 Raymond Durgnat, *Franju* (Berkeley, 1968), p. 78.

5 David Rothel, *The Great Showbusiness Animals* (San Diego, CA, 1980), p. 69; Ann Paietta and Jean Kauppila, *Animals on Screen and Radio: An Annotated Sourcebook* (Metuchen, NJ, 1994), p. vii. See also Pauline Bartel, *Amazing Animal Actors* (Dallas, 1997).

6 Boone had looked after Strongheart, *Letters to Strongheart* (London, 1940), p. 31.

7 *Ibid.*, p. xiv.

8 *Ibid.*, p. 296.

9 Polly Toynbee, 'Why Weep over Rodeo Horses when there are Orphans of Kosovo also Available for our Tears', *Radio Times*, CCXCVIII (4–10 July 1998), p. 10.

10 Steve Baker, *The Postmodern Animal* (London, 2000), p. 22.

11 John Berger, 'Why Look at Animals?' in John Berger, *About Looking* (London, 1980).

12 Akira Lippit, *Electric Animal: Toward a Rhetoric of Wildlife* (Minneapolis, 2000), p. 25.

13 *Ibid.*, p. 187.

14 *Ibid.*, p. 21.

15 James Serpell, *In the Company of Animals: A Study of*

Human–Animal Relationships (Cambridge, 1996), pp. 19-20; Erica Fudge, *Animal* (London, 2002).

16 Sigmund Freud, 'Mourning and Melancholia' in *On Metapsychology: The Theory of Psychoanalysis* (Harmondsworth, 1984), pp. 267–8.

17 Chris Philo and Chris Wilbert, 'Animal Spaces, Beastly Places: An Introduction', in Chris Philo and Chris Wilbert, eds, *Animal Spaces, Beastly Places: New Geographies of Human–Animal Relations* (London, 2000), p. 17; see also Chris Wilbert, 'Anti-This – Against-That: Resistances along a Human–Non-Human Axis' in Joanna Sharp, Paul Routledge, Chris Philo and Ronan Paddison, eds, *Entanglements of Power: Geographies of Domination/Resistance* (London, 2000), pp. 249–51.

18 Hilda Kean, *Animal Rights: Political and Social Change in Britain since 1800* (London, 1998), pp. 26–7. 'A new humanity towards the animals who lived, worked and traversed the urban domain becomes a distinct part of modernity', p. 31. See also Diana Donald, '"Beastly Sights": The Treatment of Animals as a Moral Theme in Representations of London *c.* 1820–1850', *Art History*, XXII (1991), pp. 514–44.

19 Peter de Bolla, 'The Visibility of Visuality', in Teresa Brennan and Martin Jay, eds, *Vision in Context* (New York, 1996), p. 65.

20 'An Act to Consolidate, Amend, and Extend Certain Enactments Relating to Animals and to Knackers; and to Make Further Provision with Respect Thereto', *Parliamentary Papers*, IV (1911).

21 Very little historical analysis has been done on the reception of animal imagery, the responses of audiences to films, or on reactions to the development of the animal welfare movement. For this reason one can only make qualified claims about the relation between legislation and public seeing.

22 John Berger, 'Why Look at Animals?', p. 22.

23 Catherine Russell, *Experimental Ethnography: The Work of Film in the Age of Video* (Durham, 1999), p. 119.

24 'Would that it would, would that it could, come clean, this true real. I so badly want that wink of recognition, that complicity with the nature of nature.' Michael Taussig, *Mimesis and Alterity: A Particular History of the Senses* (London, 1993), p. xvii.

25 Russell, *Experimental Ethnography*, p. 122; my italics.

26 Bousé, *Wildlife Films*, p. 43. See also his remarks about eco-porn, p. 182.

27 Linda Williams, *Hard Core: Power, Pleasure and the 'Frenzy of the Visible'* (London, 1990), p. 45.

28 This argument does not quite apply to those films where trained animals are being used to simulate violence, though even these types of scenes can be subject to complaint and, as the argument over *Amores Perros*, discussed in chapter three, demonstrates, possible censorship.

29 Berger, 'Why Look at Animals?', p. 26.

30 See Gail Davies's fascinating PhD, *Networks of Nature: Stories of Natural History Film-making from the BBC* (University College, London, 1998), p. 88. For an account of the making of *Life on Earth*, see chapter 5 of her thesis.

31 *Ibid.*, p. 172.

32 David Ingram, *Green Screen: Environmentalism and Hollywood Cinema* (Exeter, 2000), pp. 20–24.

33 *Ibid.*, p. 24.

34 Leslie Halliwell, *Halliwell's Film and Video Guide 2002*, ed. John Walker (London, 2001), p. 481.

35 Davies, *Networks of Nature*, p. 177.

36 Bill Viola, *Reasons for Knocking at an Empty House: Writings 1973–1994*, edited by Robert Violette in collaboration with Bill Viola (London, 1995), p. 143. For a reading of Viola's film see

Russell, *Experimental Ethnography,* pp. 183–8.

37 As an example of the dog as camera in literature, see Susan McHugh, 'Marrying my Bitch: J. R. Ackerley's Pack Sexualities', *Critical Inquiry,* XXVII (2000).

38 H. F. Hintz, *Horses in the Movies* (South Brunswick, 1979), pp. 12–13, 117.

39 On horses and eroticism see Parker Tyler, 'The Horse, Totem Symbol of American Films', *Sight and Sound,* XVI (1947), pp. 113–14.

40 Slavoj Zizek, *Did Somebody Say Totalitarianism: Five Interventions in the (Mis)use of a Notion* (London, 2000), p. 37.

41 Peter Shaffer, *Equus* (Harmondsworth, 1977), p. 13.

42 *Ibid.,* p. 15.

43 There are, in fact, other forms of communication in the film. Jesse recognizes Willy's lamenting cries for his family out at sea, for instance. It is interesting to note that Jesse being able to put his hand in the mouth of Willy is the sign of ultimate trust. In Christophe Gans's *Fraternité des Loups* (2001) a savage (unspeci-fied) beast 'brought back from Africa', made monstrous by being covered in a form of armature, terrorizes the countryside. As the beast lies dying, the hero of the film exchanges a look with the eye of the beast and places his hand in the beast's mouth.

44 Lippit, *Electric Animal,* p. 24. There is an interesting appreciation of this fact in television marketing. John Lyttle, the television editor of *City Limits,* noted how animals were such effective image creators. They are cute, easy to personalize, and stick in the mind. With the growth of time-shift viewing on video, advertisers use animals to create an instant brand image to those fast-forwarding the breaks.' Stephen Pinder, 'When the Little People Win with Paws for Thought', *Broadcast* (3 April 1987), p.20.

45 On whaling and anti-whaling films see Ingram, *Green Screen,*

pp. 84–7.

46 On the filming of Moby Dick see Axel Madsen, *John Huston* (London, 1979), pp. 144–60; Stuart M. Kaminsky, *John Huston: Maker of Magic* (London, 1978), pp. 101–7.

47 Richard Jameson notes how the faces of the crew take on a leprous whiteness as they come to share Ahab's obsession with Moby Dick. Jameson, 'John Huston', in Stephen Cooper, ed, *Perspectives on John Huston* (New York, 1994), p. 72. Huston managed to get the washed-out colour that tones the whole film by shooting Moby Dick in Technicolor and then making two sets of negatives, one black and white and one colour, which he then recombined.

48 In psychoanalytic terms one might describe this as a variation on the idea of the encounter with the Real: 'the Real of an indigestible traumatic encounter, of an enigma that resists symbolization . . . The shocking impact of being affected/ "seduced" by the enigmatic message of the Other derails the subject's *automaton*, opens up a gap which the subject is free to fill with his (ultimately failed) endeavours to symbolize it.' Slavoj Zizek, *Totalitarianism*, p. 58. However, the filmic animal reflects a different problem because the response to the enigma the animal presents is not to symbolize it but to imitate it or master it through imitation.

49 This anticipates the theme of voyeurism in Huston's later film *Reflections in a Golden Eye* (1967). This film also raises questions of sexuality in relation to hunting and riding, both activities on which Huston was very keen. Kaminsky, *Huston*, p. 174.

50 It is worth noting a remark of Joan Copjec's in relation to chase structures in film: 'The parallel or alternating montage that is so often used to create sequences of cinematic suspense works by inserting pursuer and pursued into a structure that makes each radically dependent on our reading of the other. Suspense is produced to the extent that the structure manages to suspend

psychology; that is, to the extent that what we know of the characters and abilities of pursuer and pursued is superseded by the technical assumption that the next image has the power to reverse all our expectations and render any psychological profile of the characters irrelevant.' Joan Copjec, 'Introduction', *Shades of Noir* (London and New York, 1993), pp. vii–viii.

51 Paul M. Sammon, *Future Noir: The Making of Blade Runner* (New York, 1996), pp. 106–7. For Ridley Scott's own thoughts about the eye, see pp. 382–3.

52 Elissa Marder, '*Blade Runner*'s Moving Still', *Camera Obscura*, XXVII (1991), p. 91.

53 Scott Bukatman, *Blade Runner* (London, 1997), p. 11.

54 For more on shooting the dove scene, see Sammon, *Future Noir*, p. 384.

55 For a Freudian reading of a spider memory in *Blade Runner*, see Kaja Silverman, 'Back to the Future', *Camera Obscura*, XXVII (1991), p. 120.

56 Sammon, *Future Noir*, p. 377.

57 Bukatman, *Blade Runner*, p. 19.

58 For Cavell, the move from doubt about our perception of reality to the more radical denial that film does not project or screen a version of reality, which would then mean we would be doubly disconnected from reality, is the point at which the sceptical model breaks down. 'Film is a moving image of scepticism: not only is there a reasonable possibility, it is a fact that our normal senses are satisfied of reality while reality does not exist – even alarmingly *because* it does not exist, because viewing is all it takes . . . But to deny, on sceptical grounds, just *this* satisfaction – to deny that it is ever reality which film projects and screens – is a farce of scepticism.' Stanley Cavell, *The World Viewed: Reflections on the Ontology of Film* (Cambridge, MA, 1979), pp. 188–9; see also Stephen

Mulhall, *Stanley Cavell: Philosophy's Recounting of the Ordinary* (Oxford, 1994), pp. 228–9.

59 The filmmakers were themselves undecided whether all the animals were going to be described as artificial or not. In the original take, for example, Rachel describes Tyrell's owl as real, though the line was overdubbed in post-production to say that it was artificial.

60 It is important to distinguish between the non-human and the inhuman. The relationship between totemic figures and the borderline of what is human is also explored in *Silence of the Lambs* (1990). In this example the inhuman, as represented by Hannibal Lector, is outside the system of substitution and metaphor through which totemism makes sense. In other words, the inhuman is not necessarily animal. See Cary Wolfe and Jonathan Elmer, 'Subject to Sacrifice: Ideology, Pyschoanalysis and the Discourse of Species in Jonathan Demme's *Silence of the Lambs*', *Boundary* 2, XXII (1995), p. 160.

61 Stanley Cavell, *Pursuits of Happiness: The Hollywood Comedy of Remarriage* (Cambridge, MA, 1981), p. 128.

62 Gilliam wished to end the film with the shooting of Cole, but scenes were added on to suggest a more optimistic ending. As in *Blade Runner*, there is doubt as to what is a figment of Cole's disturbed mind and what is reality.

63 David Lashmet notes the significance of the locations of Baltimore and Philadelphia in relation to animal experimentation. The Centre for Human Virology was established by Robert Gallo in Baltimore in 1996, and the Wistar Institute, the source of the Belgian Congo oral polio vaccine, is based in Philadelphia. David Lashmet, '"The future is history": 12 Monkeys and the origin of AIDS', *Mosaic*, XXXIII (2000), p. 68. Note also his remarks about the possible relation (or coincidence) between the film's title and the Silver Spring monkeys, which I discuss in chapter three.

2 vision and ethics

1 For other angles on the link between technology and value see
Miriam Hansen, 'Of Mice and Ducks: Benjamin and Adorno on
Disney', *South Atlantic Quarterly*, XCII (1993), pp. 27–61; 'the
Disney films catalysed discussions of the psycho-politics of mass-
cultural reception, specifically the linkage of laughter and violence
and the sadomasochistic slant of spectatorial pleasure. But they
also rehearsed, especially for Benjamin, alternative visions of technology and the body, prefiguring the mobilization of a "collective
physis" and a different organization of the relations between
humanity and nature', p. 28. Also Susan McHugh, 'Bringing Up
Babe', *Camera Obscura*, XVII (2002), pp. 149–87.

2 R. W. Jones, '"The sight of creatures strange to our clime":
London Zoo and the Consumption of the Exotic', *Journal of Victorian Culture*, II (1997), p. 275; Harriet Ritvo, *The Animal Estate:
The English and Other Creatures in the Victorian Age* (Cambridge,
1987), p. 5; my italics.

3 Paul S. Crowson, *Animals in Focus: The Business Life of a Natural
History Film Unit* (London, 1981), p.85. He remarks earlier in the
book, 'only profound biological knowledge enables you to anticipate your animal's next movement; only profound sympathy makes
you able and anxious to alter your equipment to suit the biological
needs of animals – to build it around the animal's convenience;
only profound interest in animals gives the necessary level of
patience', p. 10. The Tiger beetle's egg-laying is also described
here.

4 Oxford Scientific Films did get involved with the film producer
Harry Saltzman in 1973 to provide imagery for a film about man-
size insects. The film was never made, although OSF did design
a large and elaborate camera for the filming of the insects. See the

designs in Crowson, *Animals in Focus*, pp. 120–22.

5　The producer, Jacques Perrin, released another film in France at the end of 2001 entitled *Le Peuple migratoire*, which depicts bird migrations. This similarly involved huge amounts of labour taking over four years to make and involving some 450 people for a 90-minute film. 'French cinematic master returns with celebration of birds in flight', *The Independent*, 10 December 2001, p. 8.

6　Michael X. Ferraro, 'Angles on Insects', *American Cinematographer*, LXXVIII (1997), pp. 77–80.

7　The Charles Urban Collection, held in the Science Museum Library, London, has cuttings and advertising material relating to both these films. See Box 3/3. Urban commented in an interview, 'how we are all the time – in speech and books and comment – referring to it [i.e. nature] in superlatives, it does seem amazing that we have neglected it so in pictures'. '*Four Seasons* is Urban Masterpiece in Four Chapters', *Exhibitors Trade Review*, 24 September 1921, p. 1173. Fore-fronting the idea of the compression of time is a frequent motif in nature documentaries. David Attenborough uses a diagram of a year to explain the chronology of life in *Life on Earth*.

8　'Urban's Scenic Rialto Feature', *Daily Telegraph*, 5 September 1921.

9　See reviews of the film in *The Morning Post*, 19 January 1926; *The Bioscope*, 21 January 1926.

10　This advertising newspaper can also be found in the Charles Urban Collection, 3/3, and was produced by the Red Seal Pictures Corporation.

11　H. A. Saunders, 'The Fascination of Natural History Photography: A Chat with Would-be Beginners', *The Photographic Journal*, LIV (1914), p. 72. Champions of moving film will claim a similar failing for still photography. See Thomas Clegg,

A Revolution in the Worlds of Entertainment (London, n.d.),
pp. 13–14. This text is possibly dated 1910 or 1911.

12 G. A. Booth, 'Natural History Photography', *The Photographic Journal*, LXII (1922), p. 216.

13 My thinking on the location of the photographer in the environment is very much indebted to Matthew Brower's work on the history of nature photography, particularly in his work on hides and blinds.

14 Margeret Harker, 'Animal photography in the nineteenth century', in Alexandra Noble, ed., *The Animal in Photography 1843–1985* (London, 1986), pp. 24–35.

15 C. A. W. Guggisberg, *Early Wildlife Photographers* (Newton Abbot, 1977), p. 28.

16 Paul Virilio, *War and Cinema: The Logistics of Perception* (London, 1989), pp. 68–9; James R. Ryan, *Picturing Empire: Photography and the Visualization of the British Empire* (London, 1997), pp. 99–139; Brian Winston, *Technologies of Seeing: Photography, Cinematography, Television* (London, 1996), p. 40.

17 A. Radclyffe Dugmore, *Nature and Camera* (London, 1902), pp. V, 73. 'It seems odd now that in the beginning I selected as the object for the first camera hunts the most cunning and elusive of the deer family instead of trying an easier subject, like a porcupine . . . Of course, the explanation lay in the fact that I simply wished to hunt deer, and the camera afforded the means of gratifying this desire.' George Shiras III, *Hunting Wildlife with Camera and Flashlight: A Record of Sixty-Five Years' Visits to the Woods and Waters of North America*, 2 vols. (Washington, DC, 1935), vol. I, p. 29.

18 Guggisberg, *Early Wildlife Photographers*, pp. 18ff.

19 *Ibid.*, p. 38.

20 Cherry Kearton, *Photographing Wildlife across the World* (London, 1923), pp. 13–14.

21 Eadweard Muybridge, *Animals in Motion* (London, 1899), p. 257.
    Muybridge captioned one of his pictures of a tiger, 'Irregular
    walking in confinement', p. 51.

22 Robert Haas, *Muybridge: Man in Motion* (Berkeley, CA, 1976),
    pp. 150–52.

23 Marta Braun, *Picturing Time: The Work of Etienne-Jules Marey
    1830–1904* (Chicago, 1992), p. 166.

24 Laurent Mannoni, *The Great Art of Light and Shadow: Archaeology
    of Cinema* (Exeter, 2000), chapters 12–13.

25 Haas, *Muybridge*, pp. 45ff.

26 Eadweard Muybridge, *The Human Figure in Motion: An Electro-
    photographic Investigation of Conscutive Phases of Muscular Actions*
    (London, 1901), p. 8.

27 Braun, *Picturing Time*, p. 125; see also Brian Coe, *The History of
    Movie Photography* (London, 1981), pp. 49–50.

28 Braun, *Picturing Time*, pp. 56–63.

29 'The nineteenth century reconceptualized the body as a motor
    rather than simply a machine; its energy levels and capacity for
    work conceived in electro-chemical and thermodynamic terms.
    Late-nineteenth century studies of motion and performance by
    Muybridge, Marey, Taylor and others, were carried out within this
    paradigm', Tim Armstrong, *Modernism, Technology and the Body:
    A Cultural History* (Cambridge, 1998), pp. 78–9. Bousé, *Wildlife
    Films*, p. 42, notes this omission of animals but does not explore its
    implications.

30 There are many catalogues listing these early films. See, for
    instance, the early entries in Denis Gifford, *The British Film Cata-
    logue Volume 2: Non-Fiction Film, 1888–1994* (London, 2000).

31 It may seem reasonable to object here that seeing more naturally
    entails an increase in knowledge. But it is important to note that
    the kind of visual imagery under discussion here, particularly

photography and silent film, inevitably leads to a superficial and inconclusive knowledge. 'With the emergence of biological modes of representation, we find a historical break between observation (or image) and object of knowledge – a break in which the visualization of "life" becomes all the more seductive to the scientific eye even as the limitations of representation are made plain.' Lisa Cartwright, *Screening the Body: Tracing Medicine's Visual Culture* (Minnesota, 1995), p. 10.

32 Winston, *Technologies*, pp. 13–15.

33 Dagognet, *Etienne-Jules Marey: A Passion for the Trace* (New York, 1992), p. 163.

34 'This history suggests that the cinema has been informed in crucial ways by scientific modes of knowing and seeing.' Cartwright, *Screening*, p. 29.

35 On film and vivisection see Christopher Lawrence, 'Cinema Vérité: The Image of William Harvey's Experiments in 1928', in Nicolaas A. Rupke, ed, *Vivisection in Historical Perspective* (London, 1987), pp. 295–313.

36 Jonathan Auerbach, 'Chasing Film Narrative: Repetition, Recursion, and the Body in Early Cinema', *Critical Inquiry*, XXVI (2000), pp. 807–10.

37 Garry Marvin, 'Cultured Killers: Creating and Representing Foxhounds', *Society and Animals*, IX (2001), pp. 273–92.

38 Bousé, *Wildlife Films*, p. 113.

39 Stephen Herbert (in association with Colin Harding and Simon Popple), *Victorian Film Catalogues Reprinted from the W. D. Slade Archive* (London, 1996), p. 24. See also the listings for the very first film shows in Stephen Herbert, *When the Movies Began . . . A Chronology of the World's Film Production and Film Shows before May, 1896* (London, 1994).

40 Frederick A. Talbot, *Moving Pictures: How They are Made and*

Worked (London, 1912), p. 116.

41 The bullfight film appears regularly in early film catalogues, and appears to be a favourite subject. A bullfight film was also made by the Lumière Brothers in 1900. The possibility of an ambivalent response to a film that could be seen as both shocking and yet presumably exciting enough to warrant its exhibition can be seen in remarks from *The Era* in August 1897: 'A Spanish bullfight, with a remarkably fine bull, is also depicted; and, as Mr Maskelyne, who acts as explainer remarks, "makes us sorry for the animals, and for those who can enjoy such a spectacle"'. Quoted in John Barnes, *The Beginnings of Cinema in Britain 1894–1901 Volume 2: 1897* (Exeter, 1996), p. 162. See also p. 166. There is an extraordinary description of a filmed fight between a tiger and a bull at the arena in San Sebastián from the Charles Urban film catalogue of 1905, in Stephen Herbert, ed., *A History of Early Film* (London, 2000), vol. I, pp. 157–8. On the filming of bullfights during this period see also Carlos C. Perales, *El Cine y los toros: pasíon y multitud* (Seville, 1999), pp. 135–8.

42 Charles Musser and Carol Nelson, *High Class Moving Pictures: Lyman H. Howe and the Forgotten Era of the Travelling Exhibition 1880–1920* (Princeton, 1991). They note an important class-based component in hunting films. 'The processes of hunting a wild animal or manufacturing industrial goods achieved a kind of equivalence in these programs. One showed how wealth was spent, the other how it as accumulated. These depictions of production processes pushed the workers and their milieu to the periphery.' pp. 177–8.

43 Mitman, *Reel Nature*, pp. 9–10. See also chapter 7 on the dynamics of the interaction between the visual animal, science, entertainment and the politics of conservation.

44 Luke McKernan, 'Putting the World before You: The Charles

Urban Story', in Andrew Higson, ed., *Young and Innocent?: The Cinema in Britain, 1896–1930* (Exeter, 2002).

45 *Proceedings of the Zoological Society of London* (15 February 1910), p. 252. Urban found some favour with the royal family during this period. 'The King's liking for cinematograph pictures of himself is only of a comparatively recent date. For a long time, as is well known, he has consistently objected to them, but during the last two or three years Mr Charles Urban has been favoured with special instructions with regard to taking living pictures of his Majesty on several occasions.' *London Standard and Evening Standard*, 14 September 1909. Urban also exhibited for the Pope in 1913.

46 *Daily Telegraph*, 27 May 1915.

47 *Moving Picture World*, 18 December 1909, pp. 873–4.

48 Frederick A. Talbot, *Moving Pictures: How They are Made and Worked* (London, 1923, 2nd edn), p. 189.

49 Cherry Kearton, *Adventures with Animals and Men* (London, 1935), p. 31.

50 Talbot, *Moving Pictures* (1923), p. 193.

51 'In filming life stories it is essential that the photographer should be, first and last, a keen and enthusiastic naturalist.' Annotation by Percy Smith on a letter from Mary Field, 22 March 1941. This letter, notebooks and other related material on Smith's life can be found among the Charles Urban Collection, Box 8. See especially the draft of H. Bruce Woolfe's speech for Smith's memorial show at the London Scientific Film Society in January 1946. The BFI Special Collections also has his 1912–15 notebook which contains listings, cuttings and photographs.

52 Woolfe founded British Instructional Films in 1919 to make serious educational films. The first *Secrets of Nature* films were produced in 1922. Roy Armes, *A Critical History of the British Cinema*

(London, 1978), p. 66.

53 Mary Field and Percy Smith, *Secrets of Nature* (London, 1934),
    p. 236.

54 For a useful illustrated survey see Kevin Brownlow, *The War, the
    West, and the Wilderness* (London, 1979). On the relationship of
    such films to imperialism see Fatimah Tobing Rony, *The Third
    Eye: Race, Cinema, and Ethnographic Spectacle* (Durham, 1996),
    especially chapter 4 on *Nanook of the North* and chapter 6 on *King
    Kong*; Gwendolyn A. Foster, *Captive Bodies: Postcolonial Subjectiv-
    ity in Cinema* (New York, 1999), chapter 2 on jungle films; Rhona J.
    Bernstein, 'White Heroines and Hearts of Darkness: Race, Gender
    and Disguise in 1930s Jungle Films', *Film History*, VI (1994), pp.
    314–339.

55 Untitled press clipping on Percy Smith, dated 28 April 1931,
    Charles Urban Collection, Box 8.

56 *Documentary News Letter*, January 1941, p. 5. The contemporary
    version of this lies in the split between blue-chip nature documen-
    taries and programmes on domestic wildlife, which still presents a
    problem to film producers. See Gail Davies, *Networks of Nature*.

57 Urban, *The Cinematograph in Science, Education, and Matters of
    State* (1907), pp. 37–8. For a similar sentiment see J. E. Whitby,
    reprinted in Harding and Popple, *In the Kingdom of Shadows:
    A Companion to Early Cinema* (London, 1996), p. 21.

58 National Council of Public Morals, *The Cinema: Its Present Posi-
    tion and Future Possibilities being the Report of and Chief Evidence
    taken by the Cinema Commission of Inquiry Instituted by the National
    Council of Public Morals* (London, 1917), p. lix.

59 Talbot, *Moving Pictures*, p. 189.

60 Ralph H. Lutts, *The Nature Fakers: Wildlife, Science and Sentiment*
    (Golden, CO, 1990). See Miriam Hansen's interesting comments
    about narration and moralizing as a counterbalance to sensational-

ism in relation to Edison's *Electrocuting an Elephant* (1903), p. 31.

61 James C. Robertson, *The Hidden Cinema: British Film Censorship in Action 1913–1975* (London, 1993), p. 6.

62 Robertson, *The British Board of Film Censors: Film Censorship in Britain 1896–1950* (London, 1985), pp. 20–21, 44–6.

63 Robertson, *Hidden Cinema*, pp. 55ff.

64 Letter from S. White to G. Nicholls, 11/10/1957, BBFC file on *Island of Lost Souls*.

65 Letter from G. Nicholls to S. White, 29/10/1957, *ibid.*

66 Letter from S. White to G. Nicholls 29/11/1957, *ibid.*

67 *Island of the Lost Souls/Mystery of the Wax Museum*, DVD, (Visionary Communications, 2000). Robertson, *Hidden Cinema*, p. 56.

68 *The Times,* 12 June 1921.

69 *Parliamentary Papers*, I, (1936–7).

70 Cinematograph Films (Animals) Act 1937, Act, 1(1).

71 PCADL pamphlet, *The Scandal of Animal Films* (1933), p. 1.

72 National Council of Public Morals, *Cinema: Its Present Position*, pp. lxv–lxvi.

73 E. K. Robinson, 'Wild Animals in the Films', *Sight and Sound*, VIII (1939), pp. 8–10.

74 BBFC Verbatim Reports, *PCADL – Preliminary Conference on Cruel Films*, 9 December 1931, p. 27. (These reports are held by the British Film Institute.)

75 *Hansard*, 9 April 1937, p. 535.

76 PCADL, *Annual report for 1931–1932*, p. 3.

77 *Ibid.*, p. 17.

78 PCADL conference, 1931, pp. 47–8.

79 *Ibid.*, p. 49.

80 See the debate concerning the Cinematograph Films (Animals) Act, 1937. *Hansard*, 9 April 1937, p. 534.

81 This was a point raised by Captain Fairholme at the PCADL

conference, 1931, p. 25.

82 BBFC Verbatim Reports, *BBFC Conference on Animal Cruelty*, 31 May 1934, p. 3.

83 *Ibid.*, p. 37.

84 PCADL pamphlet, *Cruel Films* (n.p., 1932), p. 2; *Hansard*, 9 April 1937, p. 531; Duncan Campbell, 'Hollywood Shoots Horses, Don't They?', *The Guardian*, 10 February 2001.

85 Rudd B. Weatherwax and John H. Rothwell, *The Story of Lassie: His Discovery and Training from Puppydom to Stardom* (London, 1951); Ralph Helfer, *The Beauty of the Beasts: Tales of Hollywood's Wild Animal Stars* (Los Angeles, 1990).

86 *Hansard*, 9 April 1937, p. 531.

87 Talbot, *Moving Pictures*, pp. 359–60.

88 Edward Edelson, *Great Animals of the Movies* (New York, 1980), pp. 4–5.

89 Raymond Lee, *Not So Dumb: The Life and Times of the Animal Actors* (Cranbury, NJ, 1970), pp. 13–15.

90 George Turner, '*East of Java*: Braving a Backlot Jungle', *American Cinematographer*, LXXV (1994), p. 81.

91 Weatherwax & Rothwell, pp. 21–22; Rick De Croix, 'Silent Dog Stars', *Classic Images*, (July 1981), p. 11; Joseph Delmont, *Wild Animals on the Films* (London, 1925); F. Kathleen Foley, 'Hollywood's Wildlife: A Report on Animals in Entertainment', *Hollywood Reporter* (*Animals in Entertainment Special Report*), CCCII (28 May 1988), p. S10. For payments to other animal stars see Kaddie Marshack, 'Booty and the Beasts', *TV Guide* (New York), XXXII (3 March 1984), pp. 10–11, 14.

92 Lee, *Not So Dumb*, pp. 231ff.

93 *Ibid.*, p.11; Margaret J. King, 'The Audience in the Wilderness: The Disney Nature Films', *Journal of Popular Film and Television*, XXIV (1996), p. 62; Richard Schickel, *The Disney Version: The Life,*

Times, Art and Commerce of Walt Disney (London, 1986, revd edn), pp. 291–2; Tim Avis, 'Monkey Business', *Moving Pictures International*, (10 December 1993), p. 10.

94 Harold J. Shepstone, 'A Liverpool Lad Provides Hollywood's Lions', *Picturegoer Weekly*, 30 January 1932, pp. 8–9. On early films with lions see Delmont, *Wild Animals*, pp. 32ff. The crew shooting the *Born Free* television series in Kenya were given the following instructions: 'If threatened by a lion, stand your ground, look him directly in the eyes, raise a finger and firmly say NO.' D. W. Samuelson, 'Shooting Lions', *BKSTS Journal*, LVII (1975), p. 68. On *Trader Horn* see W. S. Van Dyke, *Horning into Africa* (1931).

95 Turner, *East of Java*, pp. 83–4.

96 Judith Brennan, 'The Pets of Prime Time', *Emmy*, XIX (1997), p. 31. See also Ralf Helfer, 'The DGA's own Bwana Simba', *Action!*, III (1968), p. 22; Ed Sikov, 'Never Work with Humans', *Premiere* (UK), III (1995), pp. 42–7. Hubert Wells, the owner of Animal Actors of Hollywood, who managed the lions in *Out of Africa* (1985) and the wolves in *Never Cry Wolf* (1983), remarked in 1988, 'The business was a lot of fun and very satisfying until about 1980. Then things started getting harder . . . I really don't know what the next generation's going to do. For one thing, animals, especially exotic animals in captivity, are becoming more and more a political and emotional issue.' Foley, 'Hollywood's Wildlife', p. S6.

97 Anthony Amaral, *Movie Horses: Their Treatment and Training* (London, 1967). See also his remarks on training, pp. 45ff and abuses, pp. 11ff.

98 David Robb, 'Animals in Film: Does the AHA have enough Bite?', *Hollywood Reporter*, 10 May 1994, p. 6.

99 J. V. Cottom, 'Une emouvante enquête: Les Animaux-martyres du cinema', *Ciné-Revue*, 13 December 1979, p. 11.

100 See Campbell, 'Hollywood Shoot Horses', concerning the doubt that was cast over the integrity of some films that carried the AHA's seal of approval.

101 For experiences of dog trainers in studios in the '60s and '70s see Dorothy Steves, *Radar* (London, 1974), p. 68, and Barbara Woodhouse, *Almost Human* (Harmondsworth, 1981), p. 37. On the contemporary state of animal agencies see Biddicombe, (1999). The RSPCA also provides a guidebook for the use of animals in film, *The Use of Animals in Filming: A Guide on Basic Procedure* (Horsham, n.d.).

102 David Collins, 'Animal Action', *Broadcast*, 5 May 2000, p. B10.

103 Avis, *Monkey Business*, p. 10.

104 Philip Thomas, 'Indy and the Animals', *Empire*, II (1989), pp. 63–4. The acquisition of huge numbers of animals for films is not new. Two Englishmen founded the Famous Pet Exchange in Hollywood in the 1920s and provided 1,200 white pigeons for De Mille's *The King of Kings* (1927) as well as 600 grasshoppers for a Ruth Roland serial; Lee, *Not so Dumb*, p. 93. Ace and Clyde Hudkins, major competitors of another big Hollywood supplier, Fat Jones, in the '30s–'50s, supplied 1,000 horses for *The Charge of the Light Brigade* (1936) and about the same for *They Died with Their Boots On* (1942); Hintz, *Horses*, p. 81.

105 For a good introduction to the history of special effects see Richard Rickitt, *Special Effects: The History and Technique* (London, 2000).

106 Jane Desmond, 'Displaying Death, Animating Life: Changing Fictions of Liveness from Taxidermy to Animatronics', in Nigel Rothfels, ed., *Representing Animals* (Bloomington, in press).

107 Delmont, *Wild Animals*, pp. 32–7.

108 Warren Buckland, 'Between Science Fact and Science Fiction: Spielberg's Digital Dinosaurs, Possible Worlds and New Aesthetic

Realism', *Screen*, XL (1999), p. 188.

109 Chuck Crisafulli, *'Man's Best Friend'*, *Cinefantastique*, XXV (1994), pp. 44–5, 61; John Housley 'Spanking the Monkey', *Premiere* (US), VII (1995), pp. 32–3.

110 Jody Duncan, *'The Ghost and the Darkness*: Bad Cats in a Bad Place', *Cinefex*, LXVIII (1996), pp. 35–6, 129–30, 148.

111 Marc Shapiro, 'On the Congo Line', *Fangoria* (July 1995), pp. 44–9; Jody Duncan, 'Gorilla Warfare', *Cinefex*, LXII (1995), pp. 34–53.

112 Weatherwax & Rothwell, *Lassie*, p. 31.

113 Owen Yolland, 'Two Minutes, Mr Penguin', *Empire* (August 1992), p. 74.

114 Steve Pinder, 'When the Little People Win with Paws for Thought', *Broadcast*, 3 April, 1987, pp. 20–21.

115 There is very little empirical work done on audience responses to animal imagery. Some relevant data was collected by the Mass Observation project in 1950. See Sue Harper and Vincent Porter, 'Moved to Tears: Weeping in the Cinema in Postwar Britain', *Screen*, XXXVII (1996), pp. 156–8.

116 Richard Falcon, *'The Isle'*, *Sight and Sound*, XI (August 2001), p. 48.

117 Fiachra Gibbons, 'Dogfight Looms on showing Fêted Film', *The Guardian*, 20 February, 2001, p. 7.

118 Howard Feinstein, 'Tails of the City', *Time Out*, 16–23 May 2001, p. 20.

3 animal life and death

1 Mitman, *Reel Nature*, p. 206. It seems an obvious point to make, but a large amount of wildlife footage that audiences see on film can never be substituted for by experience simply because few

people have the privilege, opportunity or technical wherewithal to see such fauna in the wild. Nor does it make much sense to suggest that one should valorize experience over spectatorship with creatures that it would be detrimental or dangerous to interact with. Bousé expresses an ambivalence at the end of his book by detaching the issue of the consumption of nature film images from the consumption of nature itself, whilst at the same time pointing to the risks of influence by films that 'move farther away from depicting nature on its terms and more toward dramatically recreating it in terms set by visual media', Bousé, *Wildlife Films*, p. 192.

2   Alexander Wilson, *The Culture of Nature: North American Landscapes from Disney to the Exxon Valdez* (Cambridge, MA, 1992), p. 155.

3   'A Film of Decrepit Horse Traffic', *The Times*, 27 February 1914, p. 6.

4   See Vivian Sobchack's essay on the relationship between the disappearance of natural death from public space and the role of the imagery of violent death in its place, as well as her remarks on the rupture caused by the shooting of rabbits in Jean Renoir's *La Règle du Jeu* (1939); 'Inscribing Ethical Space: Ten Propositions on Death, Representation, and Documentary', *Quarterly Review of Film Studies*, IX, (1984), p. 293. 'The event of death may finally exceed and confound all indexical representation and documentary codings, but it also generates the most visible and morally charged acts of visual representation', p. 299.

5   Blum, *The Monkey Wars* (Oxford, 1994), pp. 109–10. Note also the significance of the theft of video tapes of experiments on head trauma in baboons from a laboratory in 1984, which were then re-edited and distributed by PETA, pp. 117–18.

6   *The Times*, 29 January 1975, p. 4.

7   Chantal Nadeau, 'BB and the Beasts: Brigitte Bardot and the

Canadian Seal Controversy', *Screen*, XXXVII (1996), p. 246.

8   This was a Zoo-check report made between 1990–93. I am grateful to Donna Edge for this reference.

9   See Paula Rabinowitz, *They Must Be Represented: The Politics of Documentary* (London, 1994), on the performative aspect of documentaries. 'The spectator of the documentary, this subject of agency, also desires, but desires to remake history. But how is this spectator hailed by documentary if the psychosexual process of identification and disavowal central to classical narrative address are routed away from interiority and located in evidence? Primarily through an appeal to feeling', pp. 26–7.

10 James M. Jasper and Jane D. Paulson, 'Recruiting Strangers and Friends: Moral Shocks and Social Networks in Animal Rights and Anti-Nuclear Protests', *Social Problems*, XLII (1995), p. 505.

11 Two recent documentary series that have sought to encompass the parameters of animal rights issues in this way are *Beastly Business* (BBC) and *The Rise and Rise of Animal Rights* (Channel 4).

12 Mitman, *Reel Nature*, pp. 205–6.

13 Barry K. Grant, 'Point of View and Spectator Position in Wiseman's Primate and Meat', *Wide Angle*, XIII (1991), p. 57.

14 Jane Giles, '*The White Horse, Seul contre tous* and Notes on Meat as Metaphor in Film', *Vertigo*, I (1999), p. 42.

15 The French text for this film is published in *Avant-scène du Cinéma* (Paris,1951), pp. 46–50, and translated in Andy M. Bellows and Marina McDougall with Brigitte Berg, eds, *Science is Fiction: The Films of Jean Painlevé* (Cambridge, MA, 2000), pp. 82–5.

16 Raymond Durgnat, *Franju* (Berkeley, 1968), p. 17; for more on fragments see Stephen Taylor, 'Masks, Masques, and the Illusion of Reality: The Films of Georges Franju', in Stefan Jaworzyn, ed., *Shock Xpress 2* (London, 1994), p. 10.

17 Quoted in Adam Lowenstein's excellent article on Franju, 'Films

without a Face: Shock Horror in the Cinema of Georges Franju', *Cinema Journal*, XXXVII (1998), p. 44. The animals and violence theme reappears in film, *Les Yeux sans visage* (1959), when, at the end of the film, the dogs of a murderous surgeon are set free from their cages and kill their master, as well as in a film made about the abandonment of pets when families leave for summer holidays, and their gassing by the authorities, *Mon chien* (1955). See Durgnat, *Franju*, pp. 56–59.

18 For an account of the (monstrous) animal in relation to the networks of capitalism see Mark McGurl, 'Making it Big: Picturing the Radio Age in *King Kong*', *Critical Inquiry*, XXII (1996), pp. 415–45.

19 Bousé, *Wildlife Films*, pp. 136–47.

20 For more on the making of these films and their attitudes to animals see Virginia McKenna, *Some of my Friends have Tails* (London, 1970); William Beinart 'The Renaturing of African Animals: Film and Literature in the 1950s and 1960s' in Paul Slack, ed., *Environments and Historical Change: The Linacre Lectures 1998* (Oxford, 1999), pp. 147–67; for an account of the making of *Born Free*, see Adrian House, *The Great Safari: The Lives of Joy and George Adamson* (London, 1993), pp. 272ff.

21 McKenna, *Friends*, p. 36.

22 Tippi Hedren with Theodore Taylor, *The Cats of Shambala* (London, 1985), p. 154.

23 All these are discussed in David Rothel, *The Great Show Business Animals* (San Diego, CA, 1980).

24 Quoted *ibid.*, p. 54.

25 Ingram, *Green Screen*, discusses a number of other movies in a similar vein, see pp. 114–17.

26 Mitman, *Reel Nature*, p. 158.

27 One of the most disconcerting juxtapositions of loss and change,

on the theme of the fragmentation of the family, can be seen in the Albanian film *Vdekja E Kalit*, where the scene of a woman having an abortion is intercut with footage of horses being slaughtered in an abattoir.

28 Gilles Deleuze, *Cinema 1: The Movement Image* (Minnesota, 1997), pp. 114–16.

29 Graham Fuller, ed., *Loach on Loach* (London, 1998), p. 59.

30 See for instance, Alan Berliner, *Natural History* (1983); Lucy Lee, *The Hidden Hearts of Fish* (1993); Susan Derges, *Embodied* (1995); Malcolm LeGrice, *Berlin Horse*; Andrew Lindsay and Andrew Kötting *Donkeyhead*; Julie Angel, *Flicker Flutter* (1997). For a general history, see A. L. Rees, *A History of Experimental Film and Video* (London, 1999).

31 André Bazin, 'Science Film: Accidental Beauty', in Fellows and McDougall, *Science is Fiction*, p. 147.

32 Fellows and McDougall, *Science is Fiction*, p. 23.

33 John Baxter, *Buñuel* (London, 1994), p. 82. Animals and insects are also significant in Buñuel's *L'Age d'or;* see Paul Hammond, *L'Age d'or* (London, 1997).

34 Donald Spoto, *The Dark Side of Genius: The Life of Alfred Hitchcock* (London, 1994), p. 463. Note also his subsequent remarks on birdwatching and Hitchcock's fear of birds. See also Camille Paglia, *The Birds* (London, 1998). On birds and seeing, see Helen Macdonald '"What makes you a Scientist is the way you look at things": Ornithology and the Observer 1930–1955', *Studies in the History and Philosophy of Biological and Biomedical Sciences*, XXXIII (2002), pp. 53–77.

acknowledgements

As this is the work of an animal historian I am very grateful to those people who suggested films to me and likely sources where I could locate them. I have not been able to write about as many of these films as I would have liked but I hope the arguments in the book will apply as readily to those films not mentioned as to those analysed in the text. For film help, references, and inspiration I would like particularly to thank Kevin Jackson. Also Eleanor Burt, Jim and Jamie Clubb for such a wonderful insight into the world of animal training, Dorothy Cross, Luke McKernan, Sandria Rose especially for those days when we used to go to the cinema and sit through the programme twice, Karen Ross of the American Humane Association, Stefanie Schwandner-Sievers for the Albanian film reference, John Smith, David Thompson, and Tilly and Stefan Zeeman. For animal matters special thanks to my friends in the Animal Studies Group: Steve Baker, Diana Donald, Erica Fudge, Garry Marvin, Bob McKay, Clare Palmer, and Chris Wilbert. Also, for all kinds of miscellaneous help, correspondences, and ideas: Peter de Bolla, Matthew Brower, Libby Hall, Helen Macdonald, Nigel Rothfels, and Rebecca Stott. I cannot adequately express how much this book owes to Nicky Zeeman, thank you for everything. Finally, I'd like to thank all those many people who suggested I go and see such and such a film 'because it's got a cat in it'. This book is dedicated to my grandfather, E. T. Burt (1896–1982).

photographic acknowledgements

The author and publishers wish to express their thanks to the below sources of illustrative material and/or permission to reproduce it:

The American Humane Association: p. 143; British Film Institute: pp. 24 (foot), 28 (top), 114, 128 (foot), 131, 132, 152, 160, 190; Corbis: p. 169; Dorothy Cross: p. 46; photos © Walt Disney: pp. 49, 147; Hulton Archive: p. 18 (centre and foot), 25, 34 (top), 144; Keystone Collection: p. 25; David King Collection: p. 140; John Kobal Foundation: p. 18 (foot); photos courtesy of Lux, p. 193; National Museum of Photography, Film & TV: pp. 107 (top), 108, 109, 123; photos © Oxford Scientific Films: pp. 45 (Doug Allan), 89 centre (Jonathan Watts), 89 foot (Bert & Babs Wells), 91, 102 foot (Doug Allan), 197 (Mike Birkhead); photo Popperfoto: p. 127 (foot); photos: The Science Museum, London: pp. 107 (foot), 110, 111 (Charles Urban Collection), 118 (Charles Urban Collection), 127 top; photos Science & Society Picture Library: pp. 94 (left), 107, 108, 109, 110-11, 118, 134, 227 (top); Ian Showell: p. 36; Bill Viola (produced in association with The Contemporary Art Television Fund, Boston, and ZDF. Germany; photo Kira Perov): p. 39; Marc Wanamaker: p. 34 (top).

index